MUSIC FROM DOWN THE HILL

A Comic Drama in Two Acts

by

JOHN FORD NOONAN

D1572601

SAMUEL FRENCH, INC.
45 WEST 25TH STREET   NEW YORK 10010
7623 SUNSET BOULEVARD HOLLYWOOD 90046
LONDON   TORONTO

Music From Down the Hill was first produced in New York City on December 15, 1993, by the WPA Theatre, Kyle Renick, Artistic Director, Lori Sherman, Managing Director. It was directed by Terence Lamude and has the following cast:

CLAIRE GRANICK   Welker White

MARGOT YODAKIAN   Alma Cuervo

Setting by: Edward T. Gianfrancesco
Lighting by: Craig Evans
Costumes by: Mimi Maxmen
Sound by: Tom Gould
Production Stage Manager: Gail Eve Malatesta

Music From Down the Hill was subsequently produced by the Odyssey Theatre Ensemble in Los Angeles on March 23, 1994, Ron Sossi, Artistic Director. It was directed by Dorothy Lyman and had the following cast:

CLAIRE GRANICK	Lisa Picotte
MARGOT YOSSARIAN	Lee Garlington

Lighting Design: John Sherwood
Costume Design: Gene Barnhart
Assistant Director: Jill André
Production Stage Manager: Steffani Coltrin

THE POWER OF ROCK

Someone once said: "To survive we only need two things: food and attention!" Food is self-evident; attention needs some explaining. By attention don't we simply refer to our life-long needs that range from a crying baby's need to be held to a senior citizens need for water when they can't walk and need to take a life-sustaining pill? Put even more simply, when we cry, hurt, are scared, worry about our health, we need to have someone else—even if it's only one lone soul—to acknowledge us, to assuage us, offer us simple human attention.

But what about a life that aspires beyond simple living and basic survival? What about a life that wants to be special? Is there anything we can add to our original equation? I propose one word: PERMISSION. Hence, our new formulation reads: TO LIVE A SPECIAL LIFE WE NEED FOOD, ATTENTION, AND *PERMISSION*.

What do we mean by permission? Are we not speaking of that sense of good will and eager willingness by which we hunt, grab, and chase that which we dream about and aspire after. All of us, be we young or old, are made to feel special by our dreams and aspirations: the desire for money, companionship, success, love, a place near the water, a book that gets us out of bed. It's what makes us human and unique. Granting this simple notion, why do so few of us spend our lives chasing our dreams and so many of us never even take the first step? For me it all comes down to one word: permission. The next obvious question: Where do we find it? In a dream? In a drawer? In an ad in the back of a paper? Is it something we're born with?

I see it as much simpler than that. Each of us in our daily lives comes upon a person who has succeeded at a dream similar to ours. Or we hear a story while we're eating our tuna fish sandwich at lunch. Or we're watching *60 Minutes* . . . when suddenly the light flashes on "I can do that too! I can get up right now and chase my dream." In that split second when the light flashes and permission is granted our lives are determined: Do we chase our dream or do we let it die?

For me the light came on when I was twenty-four years old. I'd always dreamed of being a writer, but I'd never taken the permission to actually do it. I was a Latin teacher. I was correcting a vocabulary test. The Rolling Stones were playing in the background. Mick Jagger was whaling through "Satisfaction." His voice made me smile. The power of his music turned on my light. I took permission. Suddenly in my head I heard two characters talking. I grabbed a blank piece of paper and copied down several pages of dialogue. In that moment it happened rock-n-roll gave me permission to write. We all hear people talking, only a few of us copy it down. Since that day half-my-life-ago in 1968, I have never stopped writing. Regularly I have been afraid to start a new play. Often I have doubted the worth of a play I had completed. However, I've always found the permission to go on and it has always been through rock-n-roll. No matter what mood I'm in, rock-n-roll always gets me to write. If I'm scared and manic, it's the calm of John Lennon and the wisdom of

Bob Dylan. If I'm sluggish and under water, it's the ferocity of Led Zeppelin or the life giving force of Aerosmith that gets me kicking. If I'm despondent, it's the humble humanity of Bruce Springsteen that allows me to pick up a pencil and start scribbling. No matter where I'm at, rock grants me focus, gives me permission.

I believe the same thing applies to the two characters in *Music From Down the Hill*. Claire and Margot no matter how hurt, lost, or confused they get, always have their Bruce, always have their Woodstock music, and with it the courage to go on.

The power of rock is the power of anything. It can be a book, a prayer, or a person. Dare to use it and you will break through the wall of doubt.

The other day I heard someone say, "Everyone these days is so filled with doubt. Almost no people have any dreams left." I say no. I say turn the music up loud. Feed the dream. Grab the power. Let us all live by one new sentence. "Don't judge people by what they listen to; judge them by what they accomplish."

John Ford Noonan
July, 1994

SOME SUGGESTIONS ON
FUTURE PRODUCTIONS

As of June 1994, I have participated in three full productions and at least half a dozen readings of *Music From Down the Hill*. Here are ten suggestions intended to help actors and directors in their future work on the play.

1) The situations in all twelve scenes are totally realistic. Therefore, they must be played with a realistic approach They cannot be sung; they cannot be presented. Rather they must be two desperate people constantly trying to talk to each other.

2) The dialogue in all twelve scenes is totally realistic. Yes, it may at times seem lyrical, elevated and operatic, but it is always coming from the characters' pain, desperation and passion. These are two very bright people. They know what they are saying and they are saying it.

3) Every feeling and thought spoken by either character is totally and completely true to them. In Act I, Scene 3, Margot actually sees Jimi Hendrix on stage at the bottom of the hill. In Act II, Scene 3, Claire actually believes Bruce Springsteen is on his way to pick her up. Yes she has written a false letter, but the minute she believes it, it becomes true. What makes great liars is their absolute belief in what they are saying.

4) The numbness and schizophrenic lack of feeling that Margot has lived with for over twenty years does miraculously disappear once Claire forces her to dance to *Born To Be Wild*. Probable, no; possible, yes.

9

5) The pain Claire carries in her barely adult body is bigger then the room she occupies in Heavenly Hills. How it got there is not our concern. Her never giving up in the face of that pain is what illuminates her character.

6) Margot in Act I, Scene 5, in doing her dance to health does not have to dance well, but she must dance desperately.

7) Forget the obvious; explore the hidden.

8) The set should be simple but not overly realistic. It should be mysterious and suggestive. The more literal, the less evocative.

9) Claire's T-shirts are deadly serious and done with a dedicated love. Margot's costumes should hide and confuse and have the feeling that she is still in 1969.

10) The lighting should be humble. The music should be loud.

11) Listen constantly to The Stones, Led Zeppelin, Dylan and the Beatles.

12) Read and reread Susannah Kaysen's *Girl, Interrupted.*

13) Read and reread R.D. Laing's *Sanity, Madness And The Family.*

John Ford Noonan
July 1994

P.S. If you love rock, I love you.

CLAIRE GRANICK

MARGOT YOSSARIAN

TIME & PLACE

The Present.
Heavenly Hills, a mental-health facility
in upstate New York.

This play is dedicated
to the loving memory
of
Kenneth McMillan

MUSIC FROM DOWN THE HILL

ACT I

Scene 1

SCENE: The time is early October. A few minutes after 1 p.m. The place is Woodstock, NY (5 miles outside town) at a mental facility known as Heavenly Hills. Room B-19, 2nd floor in the unlocked wing of the hospital—2 beds, 2 desks, 2 closets, 2 sets of drawers for cabinets.

AT RISE: LIGHTS UP! S.R. CLAIRE GRANICK sits on bed. Dark, pretty, early-mid-20's, angry, spirited and vital. SHE wears a sweatshirt with sleeves cut at shoulder. Across front of shirt in large letters: WHO NEEDS SANITY I'VE GOT BRUCE. SHE listens to a Springsteen album.

Enter MARGOT YOSSARIAN with suitcase in one hand and huge TEDDY BEAR in other. MARGOT, early-mid-40's, dark, beautiful, lithe, militant and very tired, sits on bed. CLAIRE launches into riff—

CLAIRE. Every time I love someone's music, I end up hearing these awful stories about their empty lives. You know that big, fat chick who sits at the next table from us

13

every supper . . . you know, the one with the streaked hair and the tits to her knees who's always picking her nose and mixing it in with her potatoes.

(CLAIRE looks for reaction, MARGOT smiles on.)

CLAIRE. Anyway, she came by last night while you were having that long session with your doctor. She plops down on your bed, springs almost bouncing off the floor and real cool she says, "I hear Bruce is your favorite." Even cooler I purr, "Bruce is my life." *(Mimicking "visitor.")* "Too bad he hasn't got one of his own." I already know where the blimp's headed, but being me I say, *(Imitating "self.")* "No shit. Fill me in." She charges into how it seems Bruce—she calls him Bruce like he was her older brother and they grew up in the same house—which pisses me off awesomely seeing as legends are legends and that they didn't grow up in anyone's house . . . which is one of the reasons they had to become a legend, being so alone and all . . . and for the blimp to go around pretending Bruce grew up in a house like the rest of us with sisters like you and me gags me out more than all her flab. I mean, I know Bruce grew up in Asbury Park with a living, breathing family but with the songs already going in his head, well, that made his house more like a church. *(Pause.)* O.K., so she's across from me on your bed bouncing up and down getting already to bend my needle, I mean, you don't need awesome plus to reign terror on my already ravaged psyche, so just as she starts her purge on beloved Bruce, I know if he ever came to visit, he'd take me on a whole tour, anyway, just as she's about to piss on my parade, I grab the pinking shears I copped out of the sewing circle, and WHAP, I cut off the end of her pinkie! GUESS WHAT?!!! *(Laughing.)* The blimp goes on talking. I snip the next finger, the second one from the left, WHAP! WHAOP!! All she does is get louder. *(Imitating.)* "Bruce broke up his own brother's marriage . . . Bruce doesn't talk to his father . . ." *(As self.)* And listen to this *(Again imitating.)* "Bruce steals a lot of his lyrics from unknown writers!" *(Makes "cutting sound.")* Snip, I get the next two fingers. Now she's got nothing but a thumb. Still she won't stop. Still she goes on trashing Bruce only now she's singing her poison sentences like an opera. *(Imitates "singing.")* "Bruce is over the hill and totally burned out! Bruce doesn't hold half a candle to Bob Seger! I know why Steve Van Zandt really left him." *(As self.)* What can I do? The blimp is going to drive me to the shock shop. I leap up, kicking my legs in the air just like Bruce on the inside jacket of "Born To Run" and scream out real loud and for real . . . *(Imitating.)* "If you don't stop, I'll cut out your heart with these shears and eat it right in front of you." *(Pause.)* I've shocked her into silence, but only for a second 'cause she looks down at her stumped-off fingers, smiles and says, *(Imitating.)* "Excuse me, but I've got to go get a new hand." *(As self.)* Off she waddles. Talk about wackos. *(Pause.)* I almost forgot: her name's Marsue De Santos.

MARGOT. My name's Margot Yossarian. They just moved us in.

(Three seconds of a GONG SOUND, followed by FUZZY INTERCOM BUZZING. We hear a WOMAN'S VOICE over the PA system.)

VOICE. Good morning, Everyone. This is Senior Staff Nurse Melinda Kasava with the morning's announcements. *(Suddenly personal.)* Winnograd over in Section A: If you're still in bed, you're clipping the hedges again today. *(Laughing warmly.)* As to the announcements: they are simple, they are three and for those with short-term problems, they are better off neatly copied on a pad. Number one: Today is October 11th, 1994. We are occupying the Heavenly Hills Clinic here in the beautiful hills of Woodstock, New York. If you are hearing me, you are a patient. Everyone now repeat after me:

CLAIRE. *(Goes along, repeating with the nurse.)* It is October 11th, 1994. I am a patient in the Heavenly Hills clinic in the beautiful hills of Woodstock, New York.

VOICE. Number two: The ping-pong tournament starts today. You have been carefully seeded, please play your best. Number three: We have three new entries today. Be warm, be kind and be helpful. Remember what our beloved Dr. Jankowitz says, "The first step to being healthy is being kind, warm and helpful especially to yourselves. I love to start my day with my beloved Frank's words:

(A contemporary ballad[1] plays over the intercom. CLAIRE screams and puts her pillow over her ears.)

BLACKOUT

---

[1] See pgs 2 & 5 for music information.

ACT I

Scene 2

A few days later. A little after 11:00 in the a.m. MARGOT has put a beautiful quilt on the bed, S.L. TEDDY BEAR sits against headrest. Upstage is half-filled bookcase MARGOT is slowly filling from recently opened boxes alongside bed. On Claire's bed S.R. sits a large package and three letters. Enter CLAIRE in a new shirt: CHRIST, SHAKESPEARE, & BRUCE! When MARGOT talks, it is almost psychotically flat and uninflected. Also, no movement below head—body strangely dead and rigid.

CLAIRE. What's all this?

MARGOT. What's all what?

CLAIRE. The package and three letters on my bed.

MARGOT. Is it addressed to you?

CLAIRE. Of course, but—

MARGOT. Be grateful. I didn't get anything.

CLAIRE. You're only supposed to take care of your own mail. It's against the rules to touch anyone else's mail.

MARGOT. The mail lady recognized me.

CLAIRE. Recognized you for what?

MARGOT. I said, "Be glad to."

CLAIRE. Glad about what?

MARGOT. What a fucked rep you've got down in the game room. They saw me go by with your mail . . .

CLAIRE. Hold it!

MARGOT. Boy, did they tear your ass in half. *(Imitating.)* "She's a psycho snob ... a useless bitch who plays with herself in the dark ... we hate her more than our pain ... we'd sign on for an extra year if she'd not play Bruce for just one day ...

CLAIRE. They're only jealous 'cause I'm rich and from Greenwich and believe in something powerful.

MARGOT. The more mean they go on about you, the more I smiled. My silence was seriously cutting into their rage. All of a sudden they got real silent. The circle around me opened and there she was.

CLAIRE. Who?!

MARGOT. This really skinny chick with sores all over her arms.

CLAIRE. That's Emily St. John. She's the most jealous one of all.

MARGOT. *(Imitating Emily St. John.)* "I'm going to kill her from behind. Tell her to watch her ass."

CLAIRE. That's what she said?

MARGOT. To which I answered, *(Imitating self.)* "Excuse me, but I will have no one threatening my daughter."

CLAIRE. You told her I was your daughter? *(Laughs.)* I don't find that funny!

MARGOT. Neither did they. Started right in blaming me for you. *(Imitating.)* "Why didn't you abort her? Father's got to be a total retard ... she's small, mean, and totally unoriginal, derivative and boring."

CLAIRE. Hold it! Totally unoriginal, deriv—

MARGOT. Suddenly I got specific. I pointed at the two biggest and uttered my four favorite words.

CLAIRE. What four words?

MARGOT. That froze them dead.

CLAIRE. Excuse me, are you some kind of actor?

MARGOT. Next I sat them all down.

CLAIRE. Hold it! How'd you get them all to sit down?

MARGOT. All in a circle on the floor. Two were crying, one was slobbering, no one blinked. They knew it was coming. I let it come. Talk about coming. *(Laughing loud, full and totally confident.)*

CLAIRE. What'd you let come?

MARGOT. Trust me. They'll never bother either of us ever again.

CLAIRE. O.K., let's stop right here. Marsue De Santos and Emily St. John are too crazy to be scared by anyone. Tell me how you did it?

MARGOT. Teddy just told me how you did it.

CLAIRE. Did what! Teddy WHO?!

MARGOT. Teddy Bear. My teddy bear's called Teddy Bear.

(MARGOT gestures toward TEDDY BEAR on bed. CLAIRE pauses and lets out a loud and mocking laugh.)

MARGOT. Why are you laughing?

CLAIRE. Man, you almost had me going. Talking teddy bears. You're a full-blown psycho!!!

MARGOT. At 9:21, while I was being oriented by Dr. Jankowitz, you came into the room. You took paper out of your desk, began writing to your mother in Greenwich only got so angry you tore it up and ate the paper.

CLAIRE. Hold it! How—

MARGOT. You then got up and came over to my side of the room and messed with some of my stuff. *(Reacting as though to bear.)* Thank you, Teddy.

CLAIRE. I didn't hear anything! His mouth didn't move!!

MARGOT. Teddy says you touched two books in Box "B." Which ones, Teddy? *(Again reacting to bear.)* Faulkner's "Sound and the Fury" and "Sexus" by my beloved Henry Miller.

CLAIRE. This is some sort of trick.

MARGOT. Did you touch Miller and Faulkner, yes or no?

CLAIRE. Yes, but that doll wasn't who told you.

MARGOT. Then how did I find out?

CLAIRE. Do you pull this on everyone you move in with?

MARGOT. When I first got locked up back in the early 70's, well . . . every place they moved me, I'd make a real effort to talk, make contact, be a source of warmth, joy and light. I have incredible social skills as well as being one of the great brains of the second half of this century.

CLAIRE. Lady, cut the bullshit now, please.

MARGOT. The only problem was that the more I tried to make people comfortable, the more uncomfortable they became.

CLAIRE. I wonder why.

MARGOT. That's when I made the big switch that turned me into what I am today. I listened, watched, recorded, analyzed. It had two startling results, my nine hundred seventy-two days of consecutive wordless waiting: one, it restored my faith in good books, and two, it allowed me to develop my theory of listening.

CLAIRE. Listening to what?

MARGOT. Yes, anybody can hear what people are saying—but can you calm down enough to listen to what they mean? If you knew how to, you could walk out of here tomorrow.

CLAIRE. So how come you're still here?

MARGOT. Rock-n-roll is forever.

CLAIRE. What the fuck do you know about rock-n-roll?! Lady, you're more full of shit than Marsue De Santos and Emily St. John combined.

MARGOT. Considering this is the closest I've come to a conversation in almost three years, we're having a damn good one, wouldn't you agree?

CLAIRE. No.

MARGOT. I only have one rule: If you touch my books, I'll have to touch you.

CLAIRE. Are you threatening me?

MARGOT. My books are my life. I take them with me everywhere. No matter how bad it gets—I've slashed my wrists eleven times, taken poison twice, and various other—I mean: face it, it's awful hard to be here when you are here—anyway, no matter how bad it gets, I've got my books to crawl into. I love to share them, lend them, but if you go near them without permission, you'll finally learn what mental anguish really means. (MARGOT goes back to stacking books on shelf. Again MARGOT with a joyous full laugh.)

CLAIRE. Go fuck yourself.

MARGOT. Listen, how'd you like to borrow On the Road by Jack Kerouac?

(MARGOT offers book. CLAIRE turns away. MARGOT resumes unpacking.)

MARGOT. Teddy says *On the Road*'s just what you need to restore your faith in good books. Teddy, don't tell me. I know she's never . . .
CLAIRE. Never what?
MARGOT. Read a good book.
CLAIRE. Reading is for retards. *(CLAIRE sits down on bed and examines package. Suddenly SHE tears up letters.)*
MARGOT. Hating Mom only makes it worse. Being a mom is harder than pain.

(CLAIRE breaks open package, takes out cassette tape, sits and stares at tape.)

MARGOT. Give it a listen.

(MARGOT goes on unpacking. CLAIRE tears up tape and screams out.)

CLAIRE. This calm, cool, quiet talking shit's pissing me off. This is a place for the upset and deranged. Scream, yell, scratch, spit. Come on, show me some upset, act deranged.

(Emergency BEEPS. NURSE KASAVA's voice comes over the PA.)

NURSE KASAVA'S VOICE. Marsue De Santos must come out of hiding and be in Dr. Bunker's office in twelve

minutes or the car from McClean's will be out front.
Marsue: We all love you; the locked ward is not an answer.

BLACKOUT

ACT I

Scene 3

*A few days later. A little after 5 p.m. Margot's bookcase
completely full, all boxes removed. MARGOT
YOSSARIAN sits on bed reading* Sexus *by Henry
Miller. Enter CLAIRE in new shirt: BRUCE CAN
FILL YOUR BIGGEST HOLE, LET HIM!!*

CLAIRE. O.K., we were about twelve, thirteen
minutes into our session, me and Jankowitz. Now you're
brand new here, so there's no reason you'd know, but of all
the shrinkers here at Heavenly Hills, well, ol' Yanky
Janky's far away the most warm, caring, attentive, honest
and human. *(Rage erupts suddenly.)* Or so I fucking
thought!! *(Instant return to smiling and mania.)* O.K., at
the twelve or thirteen minute juncture, Janky's yanking me
about me never mixing with the other patients, so I zone
out by looking out the window and wow!! *(Neither smiling
maniacally nor screaming ragingly but "a little girl" with
Daddy voice.)* "Out the window, Doctor, Look: Marsue De
Santos and Emily St. John are playing frisbee. Oh, Doctor,
they want to kill me both. They don't deserve frisbee fun."
(Suddenly becoming Doctor.) "Cut the shit, Claire. We're

talking about your life."(As self.) "I've already got one, Asshole. Bruce is my life." (Again as Doctor.) "Claire, do you seriously think Bruce Springsteen's music is a sound basis for a happy and healthy life?" (Again as self from therapy.) "Jankowitz, you fuckin' phony, pious prick. Five days a week we meet for over four months. I share everything with you. You told me how amazing I was and what courage it took to believe in the power of one thing to save me from my rage. You laughed and hugged me and lifted me into the air when I explained how much all the music from the Woodstock era meant to me when I was twelve and my father kept staring at my tits and my mother wouldn't listen. You went to your knees and crawled crying when we re-enacted killing my Vassar roommate way back when! You've been my . . . my . . . my . . ." (As self in the now.) I am so filled with rage I stick on the word "my" for over two minutes. (Again acting out from therapy.) "My . . . my . . . my . . . my . . ." (Again in the now.) It's my Vassar dorm all over again. I want to rip out his throat, chew it into spitballs and blow those spitballs one by one up his asshole. I stop and remember Bruce. I start to hum "Hungry Heart." I don't want to get locked up again or go back to McClean's. I spit twice on the floor, put on my sane smile and say, (Again in therapy.) "Doctor, could you explain why you're attacking Bruce right now?" (As self in the now.) He smiles and it's my mother's smile so I know it's needles and pokes. Smiling that smile he says, (Imitating Doctor.) "The entire committee has decided the following: one, you can only listen to Bruce in your room for one hour after supper; and two, absolutely no more Bruce T-shirts. If you don't abide by our ruling you'll be asked to leave Heavenly Hills immediately." *(Again as self.)* He's not only my mother's smile, he's her whole game: pretend to listen but never hear. *(Imitating Mother.)* "Baby, rock's only a phase . . . Baby, I hear every word you're saying . . . Claire, darling, you were my easiest birth. Why are you my hardest child?" *(Again as self.)* So there's Mommy Jankowitz with his mommy, mommy smile, daring me to get around this lie of lies . . . which I do . . . How? Immediately flash into face number five. It's healthy, hopeful, everything they need to see. Nice, nice, nice. *(Showing Face Five.)* I haven't used it since the murder trials back when. *(Acting Face Five.)* "Doctor, I will not only give up my Bruce shirts and listen just an hour a day but I will honestly make an effort to mix with the other patients if you, Doctor Jankowitz, will honestly answer me one simple question." *(As Doctor.)* "If I can, Claire." *(As self in therapy.)* "When my parents moved me here from Austin Riggs in Stockbridge, Mass. I was very scared. They got me to agree to the move by saying that your hospital here at Heavenly Hills overlooked the original sight of the 1969 Woodstock Festival of Love, Peace and Harmony. Doctor, *does* Heavenly Hills overlook the original sight of the 1969 Woodstock Festival of Love, Peace and Harmony?" *(As self in the now.)* For the longest time nothing but my mother's smile . . . *(Again in therapy.)* "Answer me quickly, Doctor, or my next scream'll tear a hole through your lying fuckin' heart!" *(As Doctor.)* "Claire, the hour's up. Let's pick up tomorrow with that question." *(As self, now.)* Suddenly, my day's rage is all used up. All I am is tears. Jankowitz gets up and leaves. Out the window the frisbee flies, I see Marsue's fat hand catch it. Over and over

I say, *(Quoting self.)* "All I want in my life is a person who will always listen and never lie."

MARGOT. I will.

CLAIRE. What did you say?

(MARGOT puts down book and crosses to D.S. edge of stage. SHE looks out and sees WOODSTOCK '69.)

CLAIRE. I said, "WHAT DID YOU SAY?"

MARGOT. Over here. See for yourself.

CLAIRE. *(Crossing to Margot.)* See what?

MARGOT. *(Pointing.)* There.

CLAIRE. Where?

MARGOT. Past the clump of shrubs and the star-shaped rock see that flat area?

CLAIRE. Yup!

MARGOT. That's where the stage was.

CLAIRE. How do you know?

MARGOT. There were stacks of speakers on both sides.

CLAIRE. What color was the stage?

MARGOT. It was unpainted. Raw wood.

CLAIRE. Why?

MARGOT. 'Cause it wasn't finished till the last minute.

CLAIRE. That's what it said in both books I read. How'd you know that?

MARGOT. The rain started early Friday morning.

CLAIRE. Was it continuous?

MARGOT. Twice it stopped. Friday around midnight and for an hour Saturday at noon. It was muddy and wet and no bathrooms and hardly any food . . .

CLAIRE. Who played from Saturday noon on?

MARGOT. John Mayall. Ten Years After. Joan Baez, Santana in the setting sun.

CLAIRE. Hold it! I thought it was raining.

MARGOT. It was both. Sun and rain together. The lights came on. The Who exploded into "My Generation." Suddenly everyone was on their feet—400,00 people, not one police officer, not one punch thrown. Three babies less than twelve hours old. The rain pounded, people swayed, the music roared through the mist, searchlights against the sky. Next . . .

CLAIRE. Cut the romance! Who followed The Who?

MARGOT. Richie Havens. The Incredible String Band. John Fogerty sang "Proud Mary" at midnight. Then it was Crosby, Stills, Nash, & Young, another appearance by Santana and last but not least Mountain. As dawn was coming up, Leslie West wailed through Mississippi Queen . . .

(Long pause. Silence.)

CLAIRE. Why'd you stop?

MARGOT. Look who's down there.

CLAIRE. Where?

MARGOT. On the stage. Sunday dawn. Look at that headband. He's so relaxed. He's plugging in. Oh God, here he goes. Fingers of destiny.

CLAIRE. Who? Name him.

(MARGOT mimics "Star Spangled Banner" being played by a guitar. It's not so accurate as felt so deep. MARGOT finishes. MARGOT smiles proudly.)

BLACKOUT

ACT I

Scene 4

The following day. A little before noon. CLAIRE is working on her non-Bruce T-shirt. PA system starts up. We hear:

NURSE KASAVA'S VOICE. For those of you interested, there will be a memorial for Buddy McCalister tomorrow morning in Chapel at eleven. Buddy fought every beast imaginable, in the blood and in the mind. May the best of us have even half his courage. Attention Claire Granick: There are three blue letters waiting for you at the post office.

(Enter MARGOT in sweatshirt and a ping-pong paddle in each hand.)

MARGOT. Why didn't you show?

CLAIRE. Working on my new T-shirt. *(CLAIRE turns and reveals new T-shirt. It reads: FUCK YOU ALL.)* Like my non-Bruce slogan?

MARGOT. We had a doubles match against Marsue De Santos and Edith St. John. We signed up three days ago.

CLAIRE. How's it feel?

MARGOT. How's what feel?

CLAIRE. Not controlling everything you touch. Not owning everything you survey.

MARGOT. I beat them three straight games by myself:
21-12, 21-9 and . . .

CLAIRE. 21-16.

MARGOT. How'd you know the third game score?

CLAIRE. I've got my ways. How's it feel?

MARGOT. It would've been fun to do something
together, make the others think we're friends, that we get
along as roommates.

CLAIRE. Friends? Roommates? Lady, who are you
fooling? You don't give a fuck about me. In fact, you *so*
don't give a fuck about me that every time—

MARGOT. Listen, I need a shower.

(MARGOT starts toward bathroom. CLAIRE blocks her.)

MARGOT. Please get out of my way.

CLAIRE. Not till you tell me. If you were really
serious yesterday.

MARGOT. What about?

CLAIRE. Yesterday when I said, "All I want in my life
is a person who will always listen and never lie," you said
back, "I will."

MARGOT. After I shower, we'll talk.

CLAIRE. *(Blocking Margot.)* Will you?

MARGOT. Please get back now!

CLAIRE. Will you?

MARGOT. Stop raising your voice.

CLAIRE. *(Puts scissors to throat. Louder.)* Will you?

MARGOT. *(Calm and cool.)* Will I what?

CLAIRE. Never lie and always listen.

MARGOT. Since I walked through that door almost a
week ago, I've heard every word you've said.

CLAIRE. Prove it.

MARGOT. I quote from the first day. (*Quoting.*) "I leap up, kicking my legs in the air just like Bruce on the inside jacket of *Born to Run* and scream out real loud and for real, 'If you don't stop, I'll cut out your heart with these shears and eat it right in front of you.' "

CLAIRE. O.K., O.K., now what about ...

MARGOT. I quote from yesterday. (*Quoting.*) "Jankowitz, you fuckin' phony, pious prick. Five days a week we meet for over four months. I share everything with you. You told me how amazing I was and what courage it took to believe in the power of one thing, to save me from my rage. You laughed ..."

CLAIRE. What do you record it and memorize it?

MARGOT. God, it's exhausting being you. I'll do the dialogue from just now. (*As self.*) "Why didn't you show? (*As Claire.*) "Working on my new T-shirt. Like my non-Bruce slogan?" (*As self.*) "We had a doubles match against Marsue De Santos and Emily St. . . .

CLAIRE. O.K., O.K., you listen good.

MARGOT. Good? I am a perfect listener!

CLAIRE. You're also a perfect liar.

MARGOT. Prove it.

CLAIRE. Were you really at Woodstock?

MARGOT. As far as I remember.

CLAIRE. Did the concert really happen at the bottom of that hill?

MARGOT. Looks like it to me.

CLAIRE. Tell me more. When were you last on the outside?

MARGOT. What year is this?

CLAIRE. 1994.

MARGOT. Inside, outside, it's a revolving door.

CLAIRE. What went wrong?

MARGOT. March 19, 1971. I was dancing on the stage of the Fillmore East.

CLAIRE. The Fillmore East!?! Bill Graham, 2nd Avenue & 6th Street? The most famous Rock Theatre in the whole world?

MARGOT. Yes, I had a seizure.

CLAIRE. Who was playing?

MARGOT. Steppenwolfe.

CLAIRE. What song?

MARGOT. "Born to be Wild."

CLAIRE. Hold it! What were you doing dancing with Steppenwolfe on the stage of the Fillmore East?

MARGOT. I was the Queen of the Boogie. Everyone in rock called me "Lady Fillmore." All kinds of different bands were always asking me to dance with them on the Fillmore stage.

CLAIRE. Were you a good dancer?

MARGOT. *Rolling Stone* called me the greatest white Boogie dancer in rock-n-roll.

CLAIRE. You're lying. I know it. Stop lying.

MARGOT. Right now I will tell you as much as I can, and I will not raise my voice and if you interrupt even once, I will stop and go take my shower and never talk again.

CLAIRE. O.K., talk.

MARGOT. It all happened in less than two years. In March of 1969 I was a Latin teacher at a very swank country day school in Long Island. *(Suddenly in Latin.)* *Amo, amas, amat, amamus, amatus, amant.* First conjugation, regular. *Amo, amare, amave, amatus.* I was a great teacher. I knew my Latin and I had my beautiful hands, but that was all. A lot of the engines on the inside were shutting down. I lived on the fourth floor of the school—it was a beautiful old estate that had been converted. That spring I was rotting away inside and so I'd sleep to the last minute and I'd roll to first period Latin with no make-up, hair half-combed, and despair in every breath, every step. On April 12th, 1969, little Joe Valinoti, my least favorite Italian child who ever lived, raised his hand and uttered, *(Imitating Student.)* "Miss Yossarian, have you heard the new Cream and if so, how do you, dear teacher, compare the new Cream to The New Doors? *(Imitating self.)* "Joseph, dear Joseph, don't you know your vocabulary for today?" *(Imitating Student.)* "If I get my vocab perfect, will you take me and the kids down to the music room and listen?" *(Back to the present.)* Presto! Joe's perfect on his vocabulary. The entire class follows me down to the music room. Mrs. Feitner, the music teacher, doesn't come in till ten. Joey puts on side one of Cream. Before the first song's a minute old, I know it's a whole new ... new ... My decay, dread and despair float away like cotton candy. I'm bouncing and smiling and leading my Latin kids in a vocabulary review. They love it, Latin and rock. Suddenly The Doors come on. A song called "Strange Days." I leap up and begin dancing. The Latin kids are stunned. Mrs. Feitner walks in. We stop, but all the rest of the day The Doors and Cream are playing around the Latin lessons in my head: Latin and Rock. Latin and Rock, wow, a wicked mix. The last bell rings. As Joe Valinoti's boarding the bus, I grab his two records. At dusk when everyone else has left the building, I sneak down to the music room and resume my dancing. As a little girl I studied ballet and I was very good, but this new music gave me moves I never knew I had. Leaps into splits into turns, wow, Latin and Rock, my wicked, wicked mix. The next day Joe asked for his records back and I said, "Tomorrow now decline *res, rei,* 5th declension." Every night I dance at dusk. Suddenly it was April. I gave Joe his records back and bought copies of my own. Every Saturday I took a train into Manhattan and bought ten new records: Stones, Creedence, Quicksilver. By early May my dancing was starting to scare me. Rock-n-roll filled me, pumped my blood, held my bones. I had a constant beautiful smile that made Joey and his classmates wonder. I had a real secret and no one was going to get it. I started reading *The Village Voice.* On May 23rd, a Tuesday, the last week of school in the year 1969, I saw a group I'd never heard of called Steppenwolfe was playing at a rock theatre called the Fillmore East. The next day, Wednesday, I borrowed their album from Joey and that Wednesday night I danced my dancing in the music room. "Born To Be Wild" was my song. I played it over and over, found still more moves. I was now possessed. I had to see and hear my song, live and loud! That Friday I took the 8:33 out of Great Neck to the city. I took a cab to the East Village. Walked down 6th Street and knocked on the stage door of the Fillmore East. The door opens. A big guy in beard, bandanna, weird overalls and high tops that didn't match—*(Imitating Man.)* "What's the password, bitch?" *(Back to present.)* For some reason I'll never know, I, for the first time in my life, told the truth and was direct with a living man, the first goddamn fucking time. *(Imitating self.)* "I'm a Latin teacher from Long Island. I'm here to dance my dance. Where's Steppenwolfe?" *(Imitating Man.)* "Why the fuck didn't you say so!!" *(Back to present.)* Suddenly he grabs me and in all the dark, ramp and ropes, I'm suddenly stage right and no more than ten to twelve feet from the band.

CLAIRE. What song are they playing?

MARGOT. "The Pusher." They finish. Silence. Nearest to me is the bass player. He's wearing nothing but a jock and bunny ears. His name's Nicky St. Nicholas. He and the overall guy with the beard make contact, people are pointing and WHAP, the guy in the bunny ears drags me out onto the stage in front of 2,861 people, 5,722 eyes. The lead singer John Kay goes to the mike. *(Imitating John Kay.)* "It's wild time and something tells me we got a girl who wants to get wild." *(Back to present.)* The band explodes. I putter and purr and prance and make silly ... I'm waiting for the first chorus. *(Sings, loud and fierce, a few lines from a hard-rock 1960s song.[2] Back to present.)*

I charge toward the drum kit and dive over. I slide on my belly like a baseball player into home plate. I jump up and yell, "Safe!" Half the audience leaps to their feet. Second verse, more prancing and silly-silly only now they can't wait for the next chorus 'cause they know it's going to be awesome. *(Again sings a line or two of the above song. Back to present.)*

I leap and do a triple axle and landing shake like a St. Vitus dance victim. The crowd goes crazy. The band loves it. I wobble offstage and the overall guy lifts me into the air and, and ... I don't know what it is but I've finally found it. I've ... *(Having trouble breathing.)* I really

---

[2]See pages 2 & 5 for music information.

should stop here. I'm starting to tingle. Too much time . . .

CLAIRE. Please go on, please. I need it.

MARGOT. O.K., O.K. For the next year and a month I lead a double life: my Latin during the week and my weekend dancing at the Fillmore East. I don't always get up on stage but somewhere I go at it: lobby, balcony, and floor, candy stand, even on the street outside the stage door I always let it rip. August I get named Lady Fillmore. In October I make *Rolling Stone* magazine. My two worlds are totally separate. I walk in each carrying the secret to the other. Wow! My Latin classes are going great. I lift everyone I touch. Everything super fantastic. O.K., once in a while a hostile guy gives me shit but then again: "Guys don't trust secrets, they scare them . . . Whereas us girls see the absolute necessity of them." For a year and a month my double life gives me a balance, a sense of . . . what I was doing was laying the groundwork for my theory of listening . . . anyone can hear, only the best of us can listen. Only I didn't even know it. If only I . . . I . . . I . . .

CLAIRE. What's wrong?

MARGOT. A light went on. Maybe it's two. Tell me where I was. My last sentence, please.

CLAIRE. *(Quoting.)* "What I was doing was laying the groundwork for my . . ."

MARGOT. O.K., O.K.! June 6th, 1970 the headmaster calls me in and says, *(Quoting Headmaster.)* "Miss Yossarian, Buckley Country Day School terminates your service as of five o'clock today." *(Quoting self.)* "But why? I've been a truly inspired . . ." *(Again quoting Headmaster.)* "We here at Buckley have no use for secrets and double lives." *(Back to self.)* The next day I pack up and move to Manhattan. The third day in the city I find a place three short blocks from the Fillmore: 110 St. Mark's Place. I can't walk a block without being recognized. *(Quoting Fans.)* "Lady Fillmore . . . Queen of the Boogie . . . Hey, baby, I'd love to boogie you!!" *(Back to self.)* I dance my old dance but something's missing. My balance is gone. I'm a girl without a secret, a dancer without a double life. I try to find something to do during the week: waitress, counselor to unwed mothers, dance instructor at Arthur Murray's, but nothing. I am like a . . . like a . . . I still dance at the Fillmore here and there, but it's not the same. October, Christmas, New Year's and it's 1971. I am shutting down inside. Each day another light goes out. January 23rd, I get a part-time job at Shakespeare & Company at 81st and Broadway. It's a bookstore to beat all bookstores. I see hope in my books. I've always loved reading, but now I hide inside sentences and paragraphs like the terminally ill inside desperate hopes. I go back to the Fillmore more regularly and then it happens. February 21st at the final Santana appearance before the grand good-bye, the bandanna man isn't at the stage door. The new door man knows me but he won't let me in . . . *(Quoting new man.)* "Even headliners need passes. Sorry, it's a new decade." *(Back to self.)* I go back to my books. I make words my music. I buy ten books every time I work two straight days—98.6% of those books up there I stole or bought at the employee discount rates at Shakespeare & Company. I am shrinking, I have no balance, my only secret is that I don't have one. I struggle along day by day. Sunday, March 13th, I can't get out of bed at 110 St. Mark's. Finally, after two hours of

trying to hide inside Rilke's *Letters to a Young Poet*, I get
up and race uptown to Shakespeare & Company. A little
after one, Nicky St. Nicholas from Steppenwolfe walks in
the front door. *(Imitating Nicky.)* "Boogie Queen, you
going on with us Saturday? . . . It's our last appearance
at the Fillmore. It's closing." *(Quoting self.)* "They don't
let me dance anymore, Nicky." *(Again as Nicky.)* "You'll
go in with the band. Be in the lobby of the Navarro at five.
Here's a pass if you get hung up." *(Back to self.)* What a
week getting ready! Six days. No eating but fruit and
gallons of water. Three times a day I sprint full out around
Tompkins Square Park. Go. Go. Go. I'm trying to
reconnect wires, get back my legendary Lady Fillmore
moves but the lights aren't flashing back on. I keep
grabbing for a sense of secret but all I am is fears, dread and
horror. I'll be sitting lacing up my sneaks to practice my
old moves on "Born to be Wild" and I'll wake up crying in
Sheridan Square Park staring at my hands. Pages of my day
are getting torn away. I can't sleep. I'll get in a clean dress
and go have dinner at the Lion's Head, hoping to generate a
little double life, but Saturday arrives and I'm so terrified I
go over to the Fillmore at noon and stand under the
marquee. I'm wearing my legendary Boogie outfit. I want
desperately for just one person to recognize me and yell,
"Fillmore Lady, what's happenin'?" I go to a double feature
at the old St. Mark's, sit through both movies twice. It's
almost 9:45 when I hit the street. I race down Second
Avenue. I knock on the door, can't find my pass, knock
someone out of the way, rush, rush, rush and then I'm in
the wings and Nicky's got my hand and all of a sudden the
lights go out . . . not on stage but inside me, my engine
and then the humming . . . only . . .

CLAIRE. Did you boogie your final boogie.

MARGOT. People say I did.

CLAIRE. Can't you remember?

MARGOT. A seizure takes. A seizure erases. I wake up numb from the neck down. A body dead. Every light out. I really miss my body. Living upstairs can be very lonely and limiting. *(Jumps up.)* Stop now. Gotta stop. Getting numb. *(Crosses to bear.)* Teddy, talk to me. Say the words. *(Again jumping up.)* Oh God, the tingles, they're really coming. *(Crossing to books, standing before shelf.)* I can't reach up. Please find me a Faulkner. I need real, real bad to get inside a Faulkner.

CLAIRE. I don't know Faulkner! Point!!

MARGOT. *(Suddenly goes and sits in corner, holding self.)* Too many feelings at once. I really miss my body but this is no good. *(Looks at hands.)* Thank God my hands are O.K. My hands never let me down. Who needs sex with hands like these? *(Kissing hands.)* Look, they're still so beautiful. Since March 19, 1971, they're the only things that have kept on working. Oh, what lovely, beautiful wondrous hands!

BLACKOUT

ACT I

Scene 5

Later that same night, 3:56 a.m. MARGOT sits C.S. in bathrobe, tied to chair. Hands tied and wearing brightly colored gloves. In mouth a gag. CLAIRE U.S. playing with dials on stereo. D.L. and D.R. are two large stereo speakers—CLAIRE is full of great purpose and energy.

CLAIRE. Smile. I'm almost done. *(Realizes Margot's mouth is gagged, crosses to her, releases gag.)* Smile. I'm almost done.

MARGOT. Why have you bound me in like this?

CLAIRE. Didn't want you hurting yourself anymore.

MARGOT. What are you talking about?

CLAIRE. *(Imitating Margot.)* "God, please give me my body back . . . God, please give me my body back." *(As self again.)* A little after midnight you started screaming.

MARGOT. My sleep's all quiet and calm I'm like a baby.

CLAIRE. A few minutes after two you start with the moaning. It's loud and very uncalm. I leap up. I'm really pissed. My rage is flying as I start across to you. Stand over—*(CLAIRE imitates moaning of Margot—deep painful and very real.)* Suddenly you moan. The saddest moan I've ever known.

MARGOT. That's not my sound. I know my sound.

CLAIRE. That's when you leap out of bed and start with the yelling.

MARGOT. Yelling what?!!

CLAIRE. "God, please give me my body back . . . God, please give me my body back."

MARGOT. I want my hands back. Unbind them.

CLAIRE. That's when you turn on your hands. First it's only spitting and yelling.

MARGOT. I love my hands. Why would I . . .

CLAIRE. Next you grab up my pinking shears and start cutting your right pinkie. I stop you before you can do serious damage to the left.

MARGOT. Hold it! What happened to my right pinkie?

CLAIRE. Ready?

MARGOT. I said, "Show me my right pinkie."

CLAIRE. And I said, "Ready?"

MARGOT. What for?

CLAIRE. To see your body do it again.

MARGOT. Do what again?

(CLAIRE turns on stereo. Ten seconds of the song that Margot sang on page 34.[3])

MARGOT. Are you crazy? I almost didn't make it through yesterday just talking about it. Listen, I don't care what you say I said or did just before, I can't dance. I'll die. I'll have another seizure.

CLAIRE. After you cut your left pinkie, that's when you made me promise.

MARGOT. Let me see my hand.

CLAIRE. Wanna hear what you made me promise?

MARGOT. First my hands.

CLAIRE. First what you made me promise. *(Imitating Margot.)* "Claire, you've got to make me get up and dance again, or I'll ruin my hands for good. I mean, I'll cut them right off."

MARGOT. I would never say that.

CLAIRE. You did.

MARGOT. Prove it, liar.

---

[3]See pages 2 & 5 for music information.

(CLAIRE unties Margot. MARGOT stands and starts removing gloves. Flinches. It hurts.)

MARGOT. They hurt.
CLAIRE. I'll help.

(CLAIRE helps remove gloves. MARGOT sees hands: cut up, sore, red, and bleeding.)

MARGOT. I didn't do that. I couldn't. I love my hands too much to ... to ... to ... You did it to me and ... Look at how they're all ruined.
CLAIRE. Ready to boogie? Boogie Queen.
MARGOT. No, I can't.
CLAIRE. *(Imitating Margot loudly over blare of music.)* "Claire, you've got to make me get up and dance again, or I'll ruin my hands for good, I mean, I'll cut them right off ..."

(MARGOT doesn't move. CLAIRE goes to table and returns with pinking shears. SHE offers them to Margot. MARGOT holds shears in sore fingers. SHE can't hold them. MARGOT drops shears to floor.)

MARGOT. Take me to the infirmary. Save my fingers.
CLAIRE. Save your whole body. Dance.
MARGOT. My body can't come back on.
CLAIRE. Dance! Move! Now!
MARGOT. But ...
CLAIRE. *(Screaming.)* Oh God!
MARGOT. What's wrong?

CLAIRE. *(Suddenly pointing out over audience.)* Listen!

MARGOT. What?

CLAIRE. Screaming, cheering, pounding their feet.

MARGOT. What are they saying?

CLAIRE. *(Joining in with cheering.)* L A D Y FILLMORE, LADY FILLMORE, LADY FILLMORE!

MARGOT. Where?

CLAIRE. Out there. Down the hill.

MARGOT. There's nothing down there.

CLAIRE. *(Joining in.)* LADY FILLMORE, BORN TO BE WILD!! LADY FILLMORE, BORN TO BE WILD!! LADY FILLMORE, BORN TO BE WILD!!

(MARGOT almost believes SHE hears CHEERING. CLAIRE turns up music and MARGOT starts to move to the music.)

MARGOT. If I start to die, will you stop me.

CLAIRE. Dance, lady, dance or die.

(MARGOT bursts into Boogie. CLAIRE picks up TEDDY BEAR. MARGOT is a little rusty, but soon SHE's doing flips and moves that were described in Scene 4 monologue.)

CLAIRE. Teddy says you're the best he ever saw. Say it, Teddy. *(CLAIRE does Teddy "voice.")* "Bring back the Fillmore East, Boogie Queen."

(MARGOT drives on with her dancing. CLAIRE and TEDDY cheer louder and louder until . . .

WHAP . . . one chorus to go, and MARGOT breaks into St. Vitus-type dance and collapses to floor in full epileptic-type seizure.)

CLAIRE. (*As self.*) Don't die, Boogie Queen, please don't die!

BLACKOUT

ACT I

Scene 6

The following morning, a little after 8 a.m. CLAIRE stands U.C., fall coat over arm, backpack at feet as SHE surveys the room (for what she presumes to be the last time). SHE crosses to door, working down the hallway (to make sure coast is clear). Picking up backpack, SHE next takes TEDDY BEAR from Margot's bed. Suddenly at door—MARGOT—all smiles and with hands bandaged.

MARGOT. Surprise!

(CLAIRE scared half to death, drops TEDDY. MARGOT reacts to TEDDY.)

MARGOT. What? I know, Teddy, I know.
CLAIRE. I can't believe you're . . .

MARGOT. What hurts most is my tongue.

CLAIRE. You were gagging to death I had to spear your tongue with a safety pin.

MARGOT. Hug me.

(MARGOT opens arms; CLAIRE doesn't move.)

CLAIRE. I was so sure you were ... so many people are dead at my hands that I ... that I ... *(SHE has trouble breathing, needs a minute.)* If you hadn't shown by noon, crazy Claire Granick was going over the wall.

MARGOT. Unpack, baby. Margot's back.

CLAIRE. That voice is all deep and different.

MARGOT. Everything's working. I can jump. *(MARGOT jumps.)* Shout! *(MARGOT shouts.)* Scream! *(MARGOT screams.)* Whine! *(MARGOT whines.)* Purr! *(MARGOT purrs.)* Laugh! *(MARGOT laughs.)* and cry. *(MARGOT cries. It takes a while. Deep, deep down the well.)* Hug me?

(MARGOT opens arms; CLAIRE doesn't move.)

CLAIRE. What about your hands?

MARGOT. Two weeks, three. Good as new. *(MARGOT goes around room touching everything with warmth and love. Now approaches bookcase, touching bottom shelves.)* I love you, books. Books, do you love me? *(Suddenly reacting to bear.)* Hear what Teddy just said? *(MARGOT cracks up.)* Teddy Bear, for a doll you are truly fucking funny. *(Suddenly shouting out in NEW VOICE, loud, proud.)* Amazing! Stupendous! Crazy! What a turn of events!

CLAIRE. Hard to believe.

MARGOT. I came to in the emergency room of the Kingston Hospital.

CLAIRE. How'd you get there?

MARGOT. Ambulance. Jankowitz is holding my hand the whole way. We talk. Suddenly I begin . . . begin . . . to feel this . . . strange dripping. *(Imitating self.)* "Doctor, can you hear the plip plop?"*(Imitating Jankowitz.)* "That's your jar of rage. It's starting to spill out." *(Back to the present.)* It was warm . . . So, so warm . . . my anger dripping. *(Making sound.)* Plip plop. *(As self.)* I look up. Jankowitz stands there with a towel. Across it are scrawled in huge letters: THE TEAR MARATHON. *(Imitating Jankowitz.)* "When the jar of rage spills, it turns into tears." *(Back to present.)* I cried and cried. I was a waterfall. Jankowitz had to get two more towels. No person should have to carry that much water *(Imitating self.)* "It's the miracle, isn't it?!" *(Imitating Jankowitz.)* "Yes it is, Margot Yossarian. I live for your kind of breakthrough. Maybe life's worthwhile if someone hopeless like you comes to Heavenly Hills and is fully restored."

CLAIRE. Jankowitz doesn't say things like, "I live for your kind of breakthrough, Margot Yossarian."

MARGOT. Jankowitz is crying. Tears all over the ambulance. I hug him. He's so small, thin and smart. He feels like Sal Mineo.

CLAIRE. Who's Sal Mineo?

MARGOT. He pulls back. *(Imitating Jankowitz.)* "I've never had a patient hug me before. *(Back to present.)* I hug him again. I laugh. He laughs. They check my blood pressure. Pulse. They're better than when I was a kid.

CLAIRE. Did you tell him it was me who forced you to dance?

MARGOT. Suddenly we're in the limo.

CLAIRE. What limo?

MARGOT. The trees are flying by out the window. I look across at Jankowitz. I think to myself, "For a person my age to come back to life, well, it's surprising, unexpected! I'm one of the few." I laugh. Jankowitz takes my hand. *(Imitating Jankowtiz.)* "Margot, you have added years."

CLAIRE. Years to what?

MARGOT. We come through the front door. They offer a wheelchair. I prefer feet. Jankowitz hugs me good-bye. He's got a nine o'clock group. I strut down the hall of wing-T. As I pass the gift shop, I want to get a present for you. I look everywhere. Suddenly Mrs. Milliman taps me on the shoulder. *(Imitating Mrs. Milliman.)* "Margot, you ought to see your eyes." *(Imitating self.)* "Yes, Mrs. Milliman?" *(Imitating Mrs. Milliman.)* "There's a light coming out. Dr. Jankowitz sure had the right idea putting you two together. *(Back to present.)* Mrs. Milliman leads me to a mirror. I look in it. Oh God, the light!! Now I know what I have to buy you. I tell Mrs. Milliman. She chuckles. Her jowels shake. She picks out your present. Wraps it up. Pink paper. Purple bow. *(MARGOT hands CLAIRE pink package with purple bow.)* Open it.

CLAIRE. Can't.

MARGOT. What's wrong?

CLAIRE. Can't accept gift.

MARGOT. Not even from me?

CLAIRE. Not from anyone.

MARGOT. Hear it?

CLAIRE. Hear what?
MARGOT. It's here now.
CLAIRE. Where?
MARGOT. Can you hear it?
CLAIRE. Hear what?
MARGOT. It's even louder.
CLAIRE. Listen—
MARGOT. Get close.
CLAIRE. What?
MARGOT. Right up against my ribs.

(CLAIRE gets up against Margot's ribs and with her ear tries to hear the sound inside Margot.)

MARGOT. Anything? *(CLAIRE shakes her head "no" and goes to bed.)* Claire, listen . . . *(Indicates package.)* I'll leave this here till you're ready. Claire, I know you can hear it if you'll just listen. It gets so loud you won't believe it.

(Suddenly the PA system comes on.)

NURSE KASAVA'S VOICE. Everyone stay in their rooms until further notice! Marsue De Santos: Do not strike that match! For the weak of heart: Do not look out the window.

(CLAIRE and MARGOT run to S.L. window. LOUD EXPLOSION from down the hill, followed by a big FLASH OF LIGHT.)

CLAIRE. Wow! That was my first.

MARGOT. First what?

CLAIRE. I ... M ... M ... O ... L ... A ... T ... I ... O ... N. Immolation. I never saw anyone burn themselves up before. When I do it, I'm gonna die easy.

MARGOT. Just make sure you tell me before you strike the match.

CLAIRE. What do you care? You're all better.

BLACKOUT

End of Act I

ACT II

Scene 1

A few days later. A little after two in the afternoon. A conemporary rock song[4] plays on stereo. MARGOT has huge piece of paper on floor on which SHE marks out individual moves of her "Boogie Queen" dance. Once a step is drawn onto paper choreographically, SHE lifts each finished sheet and replaces it with clean sheet, once again diagramming next step. MARGOT wears T-shirt: LADY FILLMORE BOOGIE QUEEN.

Enter CLAIRE. SHE wears a black T-shirt that says: I KNOW YOU HAD TO.

MARGOT. How was Marsue's memorial? Did Emily hold up?

CLAIRE. Did you use my stencil for that?

MARGOT. Jankowitz is letting me give a boogie workshop. I'm working out the moves, step by step. Then I'll Xerox the sheets so all the kids in the workshop can practice at home.

CLAIRE. At home?

MARGOT. In their rooms! I want to pass it on as fast as I can. I had no idea it was this complicated. Intricate. Special. Amazing. Claire, you gave life back to a very special body.

---

[4]See pages 2 & 5 for music information.

49

CLAIRE. Margot, listen—

MARGOT. Special body! Special day! Special morning!! I spent over three hours with Jankowitz.

CLAIRE. He doesn't have three hours for one person.

MARGOT. We went over my theory of listening, my faith in good books. *(Imitating self.)* "Doctor, like Janice told Jimmy, you're as young as you listen, you're as happy as you read." *(Back to present.)* He wrote it down like God said it.

CLAIRE. Did my name come up?

MARGOT. His eyes get so bright. Suddenly he yells . . . *(Imitating Jankowitz.)* "It scares me but tell me about rock-n-roll." *(Back to present.)* I keep forgetting that professors, psychiatrists, professionals and just plain people in general have never let the back beat bang in their heads. To them rock is Russian. I put on a tape!

CLAIRE. Who?

MARGOT. Hendrix

CLAIRE. What cut?

MARGOT. Foxy Lady.

CLAIRE. That's from "Are You Experienced?" fall of '68.

MARGOT. Not true—January '67. Fall of '68 was "Electric Ladyland." I play two cuts. *(Imitating self.)* "Doc, can you hear the back beat?" *(Imitating Jankowitz.)* "Nope!" *(Back to present.)* I bang along. He joins me. Bangs pretty good. Suddenly we're both banging out the back beat. He leaps up. Rips off his tie and coat. Grabs my hand. We dance. He moves pretty good for a skinny guy who's all head and neck. We stop. We're gasping. *(Imitating Jankowitz.)* "Thanks, Fillmore Lady, for showing me the back beat." *(Back to present.)* I stand there.

Scared. Light as air. Suddenly I laugh. "From now on it's nothing but real mornings and regular nights." I can do anything I want. Jankowitz says I'm ready for a halfway house, but I'd rather stay—my dancing can save everyone. I may be old, but I'm a good old.

CLAIRE. I'm not old at all. Fresh. Cherry. Young enough to be your daughter almost.

MARGOT. Enough about me—how was your day?

CLAIRE. DOES ANYONE KNOW I'M THE ONE? DOES ANYONE KNOW I SINGLE-HANDEDLY BROUGHT YOU BACK? DOES ANYONE KNOW WHERE YOU'D BE WITHOUT ME?

MARGOT. Certainly, I do!

CLAIRE. All day I've been walking around. Checking this. Scoping that. The rec room. Boiler room. Mail depot. Lots of up-and-downs past Jankowitz's office. I'm pissed. Crazed. My ravaged psyche is ready for red. I deep-breathe. Reduce the killer vibes. I work my way through the rec room. Marsue De Santos is playing Emily St. John. The Blimp against the Whimp.

MARGOT. Whoa, girl—isn't Marsue dead?

CLAIRE. God, do I want to rearrange their two assholes. Instead, I just stand there and smile. Their gang of five is freaked. They've never seen me not crazed. I've always thought, "The more you're hated, the quicker you heal," but this new way's chilling me out. I leave the leapin' lesbos and BAM, I see two new patients playing checkers. Spies. I can tell. More hired actors. Lots of us ain't real patients. The ratio here is 2-to-1: two actors for every real patient. *(Pause.)* Suddenly Emily St. John slaps me in the ass real hard with her ping-pong paddle. *(Imitating Emily.)* "Girls, want to meet a psycho from

Greenwich?" *(Back to present.)* I just smile and say, *(Quoting self.)* "Thanks, Emily, a paddle in the ass is just what I needed." *(Back to present.)* I feel so great not wanting to maim everybody I see. *(Pause.)* Next I scope the gift gallery. There you are. Mrs. Milliman in your arms. Tears splattering everywhere.

MARGOT. That wasn't me.

CLAIRE. I wanted to waste you so bad from behind. But, no, I just walk up to the desk. *(Doing self.)* "Hi, Mrs. Milliman." *(Imitating Mrs. Milliman.)* "Hi." *(As self.)* "Isn't it wonderful about Margot coming all the way back to life?!" *(Back to present.)* Anyway, that's when I popped in on Jankowitz.

MARGOT. Really?

CLAIRE. He had ten minutes between sessions.

MARGOT. Wow!

CLAIRE. The Hendrix tape was still in place.

MARGOT. Did Jankowitz play it?

CLAIRE. Loud. I danced.

MARGOT. How did he react?

CLAIRE. *(Imitating Jankowitz.)* "Wow, I got two great dancers living together!"

MARGOT. I feel so honored.

CLAIRE. Next he grabs me.

MARGOT. And says?

CLAIRE. *(Imitating Jankowitz.)* "Claire, darling, your jar of rage is loosening up. I can hear your dripping."

MARGOT. Could you?

CLAIRE. Next we do the flash card drill.

MARGOT. What's that?

CLAIRE. Top speed. I was perfect.

MARGOT. How else!

CLAIRE. After all the people I've killed and now I'm . . . healthy! *(Pause.)* He kissed me.

MARGOT. And said?

CLAIRE. *(Quoting Jankowitz.)* "She was a miracle. You, Claire, are an astonishment."

MARGOT. Wow!

CLAIRE. Fuckin' Jankowitz. God bless Dr. J. What an afternoon we just had.

MARGOT. Jankowitz hasn't been here all afternoon. He left for New York City the minute he finished dancing.

(CLAIRE freezes—deadly silence.)

BLACKOUT

ACT II

Scene 2

A few days later. Late afternoon, 4:46 p.m. On Claire's bed, two letters. MARGOT stands in bookshelf, arms fully extended and locked in position. SHE can't move, frozen still. Enter CLAIRE. Her T-shirt reads: LADY PUMP. SHE is sweaty from working out. Haughty and proud. For several seconds CLAIRE doesn't even notice Margot's dilemma—

CLAIRE. Broke the bench record by twelve pounds! Two hundred and forty on the nose!

MARGOT. Two hundred and forty pounds?

CLAIRE. Thirteen witnesses. Emily St. John was so shocked her flab didn't jiggle.

MARGOT. Emily's the skinny one.

CLAIRE. Wow! It was awesome. Overwhelming. I'm always surprising people, myself included. It's absolutely incredible the way I can . . . *(Suddenly noticing Margot.)* What's up?

MARGOT. I'm stuck. *(Laughing.)* Before I forget, my boogie class is going great—thirteen have signed up. There's always a place for you.

CLAIRE. Listen—

MARGOT. I walk in the room. Plop down on your bed. I can't get you out of my mind. The thought of your life hangs like a tent over me. I look over at my bookshelf. Leap up. Yell out. *(Quoting self.)* "There's a sentence in one of my books that will bring Claire Granick back to earth." *(Back to present.)* I see the answer on the top shelf. I reach up and BAM, everything locks. Jankowitz said this would happen if I overdid it. Would you be kind enough?

CLAIRE. What?

MARGOT. Seventh from the right. Top shelf.

(CLAIRE grabs chair, crosses with it to bookshelf, stands on chair, grabs book, sits down with it.)

MARGOT. Read me the first sentence.

CLAIRE. *(Opening book, quoting first sentence.)* "It's just about over. It won't be long now."

MARGOT. Once more.

CLAIRE. *(Quoting.)* "It's just about over. It won't be long now."

MARGOT. Is it?

CLAIRE. Is it what?

MARGOT. Just about over? *(Pause.)* How much longer do you figure?

CLAIRE. My body calls. *(CLAIRE gets to floor, rolls onto back, hands behind neck, sit-up time.)* Count me.

(CLAIRE starts doing sit-ups. MARGOT counts in silence. CLAIRE stops at 31.)

CLAIRE. You're not counting.

MARGOT. Yes, I am—thirty-one.

CLAIRE. So say it out.

MARGOT. You didn't say, "Say it out." You said, "Count me." If you want numbers in the air . . . *(Suddenly MARGOT's arms unlock and fall to her sides.)* Look, they unlocked. *(Moving arms around.)* Look, they work. I'm not going to be a very good old person. Shall we resume reading?

CLAIRE. *(Suddenly notices two letters on her bed.)* Margot, didn't I tell you about picking up my mail?

MARGOT. Wasn't me.

CLAIRE. How'd they get there?

MARGOT. Got me.

CLAIRE. So pick 'em up.

MARGOT. Me?

CLAIRE. Yeah, you. Pick 'em up, open 'em and read them to me.

MARGOT. But they're addressed to you.

CLAIRE. Please. Just do it. *(Pause.)* For me. Please.

MARGOT. Which one first?

CLAIRE. Not the blue. Blue's always bad! My mother's not capable of real feeling. The other letter, please.

(MARGOT opens blue letter, unfolds several pages, starts to read.)

CLAIRE. What's it say?

(MARGOT reads to herself.)

CLAIRE. Is it a request? A demand? A denial?
MARGOT. *(Finishes letter.)* What penmanship! What a prose style. What lively emotions!!
CLAIRE. Who's it from?

(MARGOT opens white letter, reads briefly and reacts in shock and joy.)

MARGOT. Read.
CLAIRE. *(Takes letter from Margot and also reacts in shock and joy.)* Does it say what I think it says?
MARGOT. Say it out. Slow.
CLAIRE. *(Reading.)* "Dear Big "C." I've heard so much about you from my road manager, Jody Bumstead." *(Aside to Margot.)* Jody was the only girl at Greenwich Academy I got along with! *(Resumes reading.)* "I'm starting a new tour of eastern venues next week. Would you like to come along and be part of the family? If it's O.K. with your people. *(Aside to Margot.)* I love how stars always say, "Your people and my people." *(Reading.)* "I'll take my limo up to Woodstock the morning of December 11th."

MARGOT. Claire, that's tomorrow.

CLAIRE. *(Reading.)* "We'll pick you up tomorrow between 12:30 and 1:00. Be ready. I'm always on time. *(Aside to Margot.)* Can't you see it?

MARGOT. See what?

CLAIRE. The limo tomorrow between 12:30 and 1:00. He'll jump out and walk up the steps and . . . and . . . Bruce will actually talk to the front desk. *(Doing Bruce.)* "Excuse me, but I'm Bruce Springsteen. I'm here to pick up Claire Granick." *(As self in the present.)* I'll bound down the steps. I'll have bags in both hands. *(Doing Bruce.)* "Claire, let Bruce give you a hand." *(Doing self.)* "Bruce, baby. I got shit to tell you that could fill ten albums." *(Doing Bruce.)* "That's why we want you on this tour." *(Doing self.)* "No, you need me, Bruce, need me!" Margot, this is it. The killing's over. The music starts. *(D.S., addressing down hill.)* I'll miss you, Woodstock. Take care of my gal, Margot.

MARGOT. Claire, I don't think Jankowitz'll sign you out.

CLAIRE. It's part of the package.

MARGOT. Really?

CLAIRE. He and I agreed that if Bruce were ever to write, call or contact me with a specific offer, I was free to go. So, ready to help me pack for Bruce? *(MARGOT doesn't move.)* Oh God.

MARGOT. What's wrong?

CLAIRE. The blue letter's talking.

MARGOT. What?

CLAIRE. My mother! Can't you hear her?! *(Ripping up the letter.)* Why do you always do this? *(To Margot.)*

She says no one's going to show up for me! Can't you hear her?

BLACKOUT

ACT II

Scene 3

The *following day, 1:14 in the afternoon. CLAIRE sits alone on her bed, bags beside her. In far corner is a small plastic Christmas tree, a box of decorations on the floor. CLAIRE sings final verse of a contemporary rock song.[5] Enter MARGOT in T-shirt that reads: GOD BLESS THE 60's.*
PA *system:*

NURSE KASAVA'S VOICE. Emily St. John, please report to Dr. Zalinski. Repeat. Emily St. John report to Dr. Zalinski. Emily, if you do not reappear before dark, we will have to make a complete search of the facilities. Any patient aiding or abetting Emily in her disappearing game will be dealt with fairly but firmly.
MARGOT. Ready to roll? *(CLAIRE nods head.)* Excited?
CLAIRE. What time is it?
MARGOT. 1:14.

---

[5]See pages 2 & 5 for music information.

CLAIRE. Bruce was due between 12:30 and 1:00.

MARGOT. Stars are always late.

CLAIRE. Not Bruce. Bruce is the one star who's always on time. He makes a practice out of being punctual.

MARGOT. Maybe there was snow down by New York?

CLAIRE. I feel like my life's hanging over the door. Why won't the buzzer from the main desk buzz? *(Makes BUZZING SOUND; by holding nose, creates INTERCOM EFFECT.)* "Mr. Bruce S. for Ms. Claire G." *(Pause.)* You don't think Jankowitz went back on his word, do you?

MARGOT. My hands are fine. I can lift them to the sky. *(Lifting arms to sky.)* But can I aim them down to hell? *(Suddenly stabbing arms down to hell.)* Look, I can roll them. *(Rolling arms.)* Swing them. *(Swinging arms.)* Shake them. *(Shaking arms, then leaping up in the air and doing a pirouette.)* Do you think Bruce might?

CLAIRE. Might what?

MARGOT. Take me along too.

CLAIRE. What?

MARGOT. I know he's all involved with that back-up singer, but with me up there making major-league, Fillmore-Lady Hall-of-Fame moves, well, the whole focus . . .

CLAIRE. You are truly disturbed.

MARGOT. I'm going to invite him up. Let him decide for himself. *(Imitating Bruce.)* "Babes, we'd love you along too." *(As self again.)* I'll bet Bruce is the kind of guy who calls girls he likes "Babes."

CLAIRE. Listen here, Margot.

MARGOT. No matter what, he'll need to see the list.

CLAIRE. What list?

(MARGOT crosses to closet doors, pulls out large blackboard on wheels. Attached to blackboard is an oversized, lined, yellow legal pad with "LIST OF LIES" written across the top.)

MARGOT. I wrote the first three hundred eighteen lies. Look, they provided a huge magic marker. See how it feels in your hand.

(CLAIRE takes marker, doesn't move. MARGOT rolls through the first 33 pages of LIES. The LIES are clearly numbered and written simply. For example, #2, I NEVER KILLED ANY GIRL AT VASSAR BACK IN '91; #13, MY MOTHER AND FATHER ARE NOT BAD PEOPLE; #27, I NEVER SLEPT WITH ELVIS PRESLEY, JAMES BROWN, MICKEY MANTLE OR AL PACINO.)

MARGOT. I'll do anything you need. Hug you, kiss you. Read you Robert Frost. Stand by the door. Sit on the john. Smile. Turn cartwheels. Boogie down. Stand by the window and hear the music from down the hill. All that matters is that I'll be here. Faithful. Ready. Available. Weaving one continuous warm smile . . . as long as you make that magic marker move.

CLAIRE. Look! I can see the limo now. *(Pointing over audience.)* There's a tie-up at the Tappanzee Bridge. *(Jumping and pointing.)* Look, he's picked up his cellular phone. Two rings and he'll reach the desk downstairs. Margot, any second our buzzer'll be buzzing.

MARGOT. Claire, we only have until three o'clock. Then they take you away from here.

CLAIRE. Nice try. I'm too sick to scare.

MARGOT. I just left Jankowitz. There are these two, big, bald guys in jackets. Club ties. White socks. Black oxfords.

CLAIRE. What do they call themselves?!

MARGOT. B.S. Quigley and J. J. Myerson.

CLAIRE. Not them again!

MARGOT. They want to take you back to Boston McClean's. They have a straight jacket ready.

CLAIRE. What did they say?

MARGOT. *(As self.)* I said, "Sir, I'm a miracle, and most of it can be attributed to Claire Granick." Baldie #1 pipes up. *(As Baldie #1.)* "The more she helps others, the sicker Claire gets." *(Again as self.)* Immediately I say, "If I get Claire to list and admit all three hundred and eighteen lies she's told me, will you let her stay with me?" *(As Baldie #2.)* "We doubt you can do much." *(As self.)* "I'd like to try." *(As Baldie #1.)* "Dr. Jankowitz?" *(As self.)* Jankowitz pipes up: *(Imitating Jankowtiz.)* "Tell Claire: Be a miracle. Don't die. Give up the lie." *(Pause; as self.)* Would you?

CLAIRE. What?!

MARGOT. Go to the board. Make your hand do my mouth!! *(Dictating.)* I . . .

CLAIRE. *(Repeating and writing on board.)* I . . .

MARGOT. . . . wrote . . .

CLAIRE. . . . wrote . . .

MARGOT. . . . the . . .

CLAIRE. . . . the . . .

MARGOT. . . . letter . . .

CLAIRE. . . . letter . . .

MARGOT. . . . from Bruce and forged his name.

BLACKOUT

ACT II

Scene 4

A few days later. U.L. MARGOT works on putting decorations on plastic Christmas tree. SHE is all smiles and hope. D.R. CLAIRE sits on bed staring at cassette player in lap. Scattered around her is colorful Christmas wrapping that cassette came in. Long silence . . .

MARGOT. Press PLAY. *(No response.)* Press PLAY. *(MARGOT has to cross over and press PLAY. Brief seconds, VOICES heard.)*

VOICE #1 *(MOMMY.)*. Darling, that's quite enough. I know you think I'm the biggest bitch who ever lived, but one last time my head gives in to my heart. Dr. Jankowitz . . . oh, where are the Christians in medicine these days? . . . in that sneaky little voice said he thought it would be a risky but worthwhile experiment to have you come home for Christmas in Greenwich, to face the real truth of what is going on in our lives.

(CLAIRE jumps up and turns the tape off, pissed.)

MARGOT. Claire, your mother's much more interesting than you led me to believe.

CLAIRE. Enough!

MARGOT. It's only the beginning. *(MARGOT presses PLAY.)*

VOICE #1 (*MOMMY*). I don't like telling the truth, I leave that to the Jewish. You were a wonderful child until you began to walk and talk, but I have been terrified of you ever since first grade at Greenwich Academy when you said, "Mommy, is everyone's pain the same size?" All your life you've had thoughts and fears and dreams I have no answers to, nor even the slightest comprehension of. I know you came out of me, but I must be honest, I don't know who put you in me. You are a special, amazing, impossible child, with a brain beyond describing. If you're willing to, I'll try one more time. I ask three favors: No fake tattoos, no provocative T-shirts, and please, wear long white gloves over the multitude of accidents. See you on the 21st. Love from a mother without a clue, Christian or otherwise.

(*We hear a few seconds of a hard rock song from the 1960s.[6]*)

VOICE #2 (*NONNIE*). Grandma Nonnie here. Your music scares me, but every day I learn another song. Back in my day, there wasn't music where you could put your hate and your hurt. I'm starting to see, Claire. However, the more I see, the more I cry. I have known some great pain in my recent illnesses, but how can a young body like yours hold so much? If there's an answer, my money will provide it. P.S., a wonderful sound person of the Syrian persuasion has installed a new rock-n-roll speaker system in the west wing. In spite of your inhibited mother, we're really going to boogie down Christmas day. I can't wait to see you. Donna Karan is designing me a rock-n-roll dress

---

[6]See pages 2 & 5 for music information.

for New Year's Eve. *(SHE breaks down.)* I'm eighty-one. I haven't cried since I was sixty-six. Suddenly I'm a flood. Please know that this great house, this mansion that everyone stops along Round Hill Road to look at, breathes easier now that you're returning.

MARGOT. Now that's a real Boogie Queen. Don't even *think* "no,"—we're going.

CLAIRE. I'll go. I'll get in the car. Actually I love limos. Limos are life. So we're in our limo heading home only first we take that road over there down to the bottom of that hill. We get out and check around and see if we see any evidence of Woodstock '69. If there is, I'd love to be able to tell everybody in Greenwich that the place where I'm getting better is atop a hill that overlooks the sight of Woodstock '69. Also, if it's O.K. with you, I'd like to be able to mention the store we're starting up together.

MARGOT. Come again?

CLAIRE. We're calling it THE POWER-OF-ROCK BOOK & MUSIC STORE. We'll be in downtown Woodstock.

MARGOT. Hold it—

CLAIRE. Know that pretty shop along the river right where Tinker Street goes right and heads up towards Bearsville? Well, across from there, across the bridge . . . there's a whole building to rent. I saw the sign when they brought me here in the spring. I know that sign's still up. You could give your boogie workshops, and me, I could rattle on about the history of rock. I could give a whole course in BRUCEOLOGY . . .

MARGOT. What about your list of lies?

CLAIRE. What?

MARGOT. We only got up to #102 lies with the blackboard. If you haven't made up a complete list, Jankowitz won't let you and me go home for Christmas.

CLAIRE. What's up? *(Different second voice.)* Everything's down.

MARGOT. Claire, what's going on?

CLAIRE. Guess what Shakespeare told me the other day out in front of the weight room. *(Imitating Shakespeare.)* "Babes, hold on tight. Youth is always right." *(As self.)* He rhymes too much.

MARGOT. Claire, don't!

CLAIRE. Your bed just moved. Why'd your bed just move?

MARGOT. I'll call someone.

CLAIRE. Would you care to see my breasts? I have three. Both work . . . *(Offering hand to Margot.)* Hi, I'm Margot. You must be Claire. *(MARGOT pulls hand away.)* When did you first know I was a turkey? *(Suddenly CLAIRE does the miraculous: a deft imitation of a turkey sounds, movements, etc.)* Gobble! Gobble! Gobble! *(Talking as though to other people in room.)* They want me to go home to Greenwich so they can cook me up for Christmas. I'm too smart. I'll survive my beheading. *(Around and around the room CLAIRE races as TURKEY. SHE picks up TEDDY BEAR, hurls back on bed.)* I'm too sick to go anywhere. *(Rushing up to Margot.)* Get better all you want . . . only leave me out of it. Too many of you are trying to get better. Health has become the great sickness of our time. I do not want to get better. It's real, real important some of us get worse. *(Suddenly stops being TURKEY and rushes D.S. to look over audience.)* Look, it's Hendrix! "Purple Haze" is my fave. Hear him? Hear him?

(Pause.)

MARGOT. Claire, they'll put you in the locked wing. It's the shock shop, seven days a week. Double doses of stellazine. They'll move someone in to take your place. Ship you off to McClean's.

CLAIRE. Fuck McClean's. Fuck Boston!! Fuck. Fuck. I'm not going anywhere.

MARGOT. Just show me the whole list. *(MARGOT reaches out to Claire expecting List of Lies.)*

CLAIRE. I never expected this from someone who was at Woodstock. Is this the kind of shit you did to each other the whole four days? Is 1969 some lie? Is the Fillmore East a total hype? Is everyone from the '60s a suck-up dead beat? Is this . . . this the way . . . you . . . *(CLAIRE races over to bed, reaches under and produces two oversized legal pads. SHE leads MARGOT to her bed, sits her down, puts pad in her lap.)* Two pads, seventy-nine sheets, both sides filled.

MARGOT. *(Checking end of second pad.)* Two thousand seven hundred eighteen LIES! THAT'S GREAT!!

CLAIRE. Slow! That's my pain.

(MARGOT slows down rate of reading.)

CLAIRE. I needed that many 'cause I'm so pissed at all of you. I see you people dead and dismembered, mutilated and oozing, the ground all red with chucked-up guts, 'cause if I didn't, my beast would leap out of my neck and actually do it. (*CLAIRE holds neck and HISSES as though to make sound of beast.*) Do you understand what I'm saying? By pretending someone's dead, you don't have to kill them anymore! That way the beast sits a little quieter—all my lies to save all your lives. (*Yelling out.*) My lies are all I've got! The one thing I can count on! The one clue that holds the pieces!! The one bolt that keeps the cage door locked so the beast can't . . .

(*MARGOT hands the two oversized pads back to CLAIRE.*)

CLAIRE. Aren't you going to read the rest?
MARGOT. Kid, this means we go home for Christmas.
CLAIRE. (*Hugging pads.*) Oh, Bruce, Bruce, Bruce, come save me, Bruce! Don't let them take me to Greenwich. Bruce, please come stay with me and help me get sicker.

BLACKOUT

ACT II

Scene 5

A week later. The "appointed day" for going home to Greenwich for Christmas. Bags and suitcases by the door. MARGOT wears a T-shirt that says: HOME TO GREENWICH FOR X-MAS. SHE is dressing TEDDY in one identical to hers. SHE hums a little of the Stones' "You Can's Always Get What You Want."

MARGOT. Teddy, got to look perfect for Greenwich. Oh, Teddy, Teddy, can't you just see us shopping on Greenwich Avenue? The sixties are back, so we can get all kinds of old-fashioned clothes. I'll get you a pair of mini-overalls like the big guy from the stage door of the Fillmore, and I'll get a new Boogie dress. We'll drive up and down, play the old music loud, give all these dysfunctional kids some hope. Teddy, no more in and outs. The revolving door is over. The inside and the outside aren't the same. We're going out, and we're staying out. We're going to have our first-rate Christmas on the outside and hang with Nonnie. She's the coolest octogenarian I never met. And then we'll come back here and finally get it right. Jankowitz says I'm finally ready to get it right. *(Pause.)* Teddy, why are you looking at me like that? I'm starting to fly, Teddy. I need a pilot. There's nothing we can't do if you fly the big plane straight and true. *(Suddenly smashing bear across face.)* I don't care what happened then. Teddy. It wasn't '81, it was '84. October 11. The halfway house in San Francisco. That guy who said he know the Psychedelic Furs and wanted me to dance with them was a goddamn liar. He never showed. *(Pause.)* That's not true, Teddy. I have a perfect memory. It was you who panicked, not me. What's happening here, Teddy? I love you like my kid, but I'll leave you behind if you can't keep up. We're ready now, Teddy. The plane's gassed, we're taxiing down the runway. You got to pull the goddamn lift lever. Teddy . . . *(Pause.)* Teddy, do you want to go out and never come back in? Say it Teddy, say it. *(TEDDY doesn't answer.)* When you're ready to go, Teddy, just yell. Mama's got perfect ears. *(MARGOT crosses and knocks on bathroom door.)* Claire? *(No response.)* Claire? The car will be here any minute.

CLAIRE. One second.

MARGOT. *(Again knocking on door.)* Claire, come on. Claire, I'm turning numb!

(Door to bathroom swings open and enter CLAIRE. SHE is dressed from head to toe in TURKEY FEATHERS. Only her arms are exposed. In one arm SHE carries a SHARP-LOOKING KNIFE. Without a word, SHE transforms into TURKEY—prancing around room— "GOBBLE, GOBBLE, GOBBLE.")

CLAIRE. You guys have your PLIP PLOP. I have my SLASH, SUCK and SPIT. *(With knife CLAIRE cuts into her own arm. SHE covers the cut with her mouth, sucks blood from wound, and spits the blood into air.)* I've had enough. Time to get bad. Time to drop the curtain. Time to dig the hole. SLASH. *(Again repeating cut into arm.)* SUCK *(Again covering cut with mouth, sucking blood from wound.)* SPIT. *(Again spitting blood into air.)* Merry Christmas, Teddy. Happy New Year, Claire. Too many of you are trying to get better. Health has become the great sickness of our time. I do not . . .

MARGOT. You've already done that speech. *(Answering to bear.)* You're right, Teddy. See even Teddy remembers.

CLAIRE. Teddy can't talk. Teddy's made up!

MARGOT. Teddy says the cracks are showing.

CLAIRE. Shut him up!

MARGOT. He wants to know how come you're making such shallow cuts. *(In response to the bear again.)* Teddy says hand him the knife. He'll show you how to "SLASH." *(MARGOT starts toward Claire with TEDDY, holding him as though HE were truly alive.)* GOBBLE, GOBBLE, GOBBLE.

CLAIRE. Stop. I'm the turkey.

MARGOT. Oh, do we want you dead and gone, you sore, you pimple, you creepy crud!

CLAIRE. You don't scare me one bit.

MARGOT. So, hand Teddy the knife.

CLAIRE. I'll kill my own self.

MARGOT. *(Suddenly begins to shake—her left hand locks for a second.)* Put the knife in deep. End it all. Remove the poison. Save us, please. Disinfect this hospital. Purify Woodstock. Save the valley. Sanctify the state. Scrape the shit off the whole Western world. Give me the damn knife, now!

CLAIRE. Go on, do it.

(Suddenly CLAIRE hands knife to MARGOT. MARGOT stands there, knife in hand, not moving.)

CLAIRE. Do it, do it. In my heart. In my heart.

(MARGOT raises knife over head to kill Claire. SHE can't. A second time. Can't. Next MARGOT races to front of stage and hurls knife down the hill. Next MARGOT lets out an horrendous CRY. Suddenly, as if on their own power, both her arms stab straight up into the air. For five seconds SHE is frozen statue-still. Suddenly MARGOT's limbs unlock.)

MARGOT. Don't you see the sin?

CLAIRE. What?

MARGOT. Can't you hear the howling?

CLAIRE. Where?

MARGOT. The Woodstock people at the bottom of the hill.

CLAIRE. What are they saying?

(MARGOT listens down the hill.)

CLAIRE. Say what they're saying!

(MARGOT continues to listen down the hill. CLAIRE is getting very rattled.)

CLAIRE. If you don't say what they're saying, I'll . . .

MARGOT. Give me a piece of paper—they're talking fast. *(Writing furiously on the pad.)* Claire Granick: You are the stupidest great person since Janis.

CLAIRE. What?

MARGOT. She did the same thing. Killing herself because she didn't like the way the world was, because people didn't go along. Letting little people reduce her bigness. Worring about what the midgets think. It's what killed rock, what killed the spirit of Woodstock. Little worms telling eagles how to fly. Kid, look at me. I'm a used car, I'm a used pair of fucking shoes. The closest I ever came was the Fillmore stage, and that wasn't major league. You got to say "fuck" to everyone. Anybody can be small. It takes a lot of work to be big. Every time they tell you you're dysfunctional, tell them, "Fuck off, Baby—I'm going flying." Do you want to be big, kid?

CLAIRE. Yes, but all these people . . .

MARGOT. Forget the other people, you're an eagle. You're a Cadillac, you're a song off one of Bruce's albums. Live up to it!

CLAIRE. You're lying to me! I'm a piece of shit! I want to die!

MARGOT. Then fucking do it! You embarrass me. I love rock too much to piss away one more minute on you! Sing a new song or fuck off!

CLAIRE. You really want me to do it?

MARGOT. I want you dead so bad I can taste it.

CLAIRE. You are so mean and vicious.

MARGOT. I'm the Queen of the Boogie. How do you think I got there?

(CLAIRE tries to stab herself without the knife. Next SHE tears a piece off turkey costume and tries to strangle herself. Nothing works)

MARGOT. Want some help?

CLAIRE. You . . . you   . . .

MARGOT. How's it feel??

CLAIRE. You . . .

MARGOT. How's it feel?

CLAIRE. (*Suddenly lets out horrendous screams, one after the other. It is the first sign of any breakthrough.*) I WILL KILL YOU IF YOU DON'T LET ME DIE.

MARGOT. Again.

CLAIRE. I WILL KILL YOU IF YOU DON'T LET ME DIE.

MARGOT. Again.
CLAIRE. I WILL . . . I WILL . . . PLEASE LET
ME . . . PLEASE LET ME . . .
MARGOT. How's it feel?

*(More and more HOWLS from CLAIRE. Suddenly SHE
collapses into Margot's arms.)*

MARGOT. Can you hear it?
CLAIRE. Hear what?
MARGOT. I can.
CLAIRE. What?
MARGOT. It's begun.

(THEY huddle together very tightly.)

MARGOT. Listen.
CLAIRE. That's me?

(THEY listen to "dripping.")

CLAIRE. PLIP PLOP . . . PLIP PLOP. (*Listening
on.*) Hey, I got my own.

*(CLAIRE's crying starts. MARGOT pulls out towel
marked TEAR MARATHON. CLAIRE cries into it.
MARGOT takes out second towel and covers Claire's
slash marks.)*

(Over PA system:)

NURSE KASAVA'S VOICE. This is Senior Staff Nurse Melinda Kasava reading Dr. Jankowitz's Christmas message. Ladies and gentlemen here at Heavenly Hills: This has been my proudest year yet. Merry Christmas, Happy Holiday greetings and may the New Year find several of you happy and healthy on the outside.

MARGOT. Hey kid, it's limo time.

(A rockin' Christmas song plays.[7])

BLACKOUT

ACT II

Scene 6

Several weeks later, the New Year. First few days of January. The room remains the same except that over the door hang two holiday signs: "Welcome Back Wacky," "Happy New Year Sneaky." CLAIRE enters first, removes jacket, manic, wide-eyed, bouncy. SHE spots signs. Enter MARGOT, calm and easy—

CLAIRE. Look, Marsue and Emily can't stop. I love it. I love it. I love it. Being the center of everyone's hate.

(Hidden behind back, MARGOT clicks the clicker.)

---

[7]See pages 2 & 5 for music information.

CLAIRE. There's another. Fuck it. A whole New Year and a whole new life.

(Suddenly noticing Jankowitz's present against wall. Again MARGOT clicks clicker. CLAIRE laughs.)

CLAIRE. Sometimes when I get really . . . really . . . like I am now, I can stand here and really hear it. Hear the music from down the hill. It's the summer, eight months from now, and down the hill plays this concert we call Woodstock Twenty-five, seeing that it's, you know, twenty-two years after the original. All the old music still cooks. Joplin. Credence. Santana. Hendrix. For the ones that are dead, we get look-alike actors to stand in. You do Hendrix so well, maybe with a wig you'd like to try out. So the music's playing and everyone's listening and then at the dawn of the second day, we stun the crowd with the new Woodstock stuff, you know Woodstock Twenty-five: Smashing Pumpkins, Pearl Jam, The Violent Femmes, and of course, high noon in the blazing heat, on comes Bruce. He plays a few okay numbers and then he does a smokin' "Tenth Avenue Freeze Out." The crowd's going crazy. Bruce raises his hand like a preacher. *(Imitating Bruce.)* "Ladies and gentlemen, I'd like to introduce to you the young lady from up the hill who made Woodstock Twenty-five possible." I come forward and I raise my hand, and like four hundred or five hundred thousand people go crazy. I'm really shook, but I'm still cool enough to look up here and see everyone on the balcony. You guys will wave, but most importantly your smiles will be lit with hope 'cause if someone as sick as

me in a few short months can get a whole incredible
revival concert together, well, look out. Like Jankowitz is
always saying in Tuesday afternoon rehab, "The power of
example is everything."

(Again MARGOT clicks her clicker.)

CLAIRE. I know it's you. *(Again more clicking.)*
Fucking stop it now. *(Another click.)* Look at us. You.
Me. We're the first whoever got to go home for Christmas.
No one before us ever got to go. Look how great I did up
in Greenwich. Wasn't I amazing? Wasn't I great? What
about my mom's tears? Christmas Eve, when I told her it
wasn't her fault. That I was just born with too much back
beat in my head. And the lovely presents I gave Muffy and
Timmy. And all the homeless kids I danced with at the
party at the boy's club. Yes, I am an eagle. Yes, I am a jet
plane. Margot, you were right, right, right. Margot, I did
as good as I look. Perfect is as perfect dresses.
  MARGOT. What about Christmas Eve with your
brother's kid Sookie, giving her the beautiful rum cake and
saying, "I made it in Baking Class for you."
  CLAIRE. It made her feel so great. "Look what Aunt
Claire made for me in Cooking Class!"
  MARGOT. But you didn't make it.
  CLAIRE. So what?
  MARGOT. When you lie to people to make them feel
better, all you do is keep them away. Like just before
crossing the Tappanzee Bridge and you told the limo driver
that crap about you and Bruce . . .
  CLAIRE. But it made him feel great! There's lies that
hurt and lies that help! Help lies are fine! Part of being an

eagle is making worms feel better. *(Again click, clicking.)* If you click that clicker one more time, I'll . . . I'll . . .

(MARGOT crosses to closet and puts on winter parka.)

CLAIRE. It's lights out in less than half an hour. Where you going?

(MARGOT crosses to closet and returns with suitcase.)

CLAIRE. What the hell's going on here?
MARGOT. We've got about six minutes. In about four minutes they'll give me two long beeps; and then in two more they'll give me two short beeps. Two short means the car is ready to take me.
CLAIRE. Ready to take you where?

(MARGOT crosses to closet and returns with a large box. On side of box is written the following: "Margot Yossarian, c/o Power-of-Rock Book & Music Store, 116 Tinker Street, Woodstock, New York 12329.")

CLAIRE. *(Reads from box.)* The Power of Rock. I made it up. It doesn't exist.

(MARGOT crosses quickly to closet and returns with two more boxes—same address scrawled large across sides of each.)

MARGOT. When they come to pack tomorrow, will you tell them two shelves per box. The top two shelves are A, the middle two, B, and so on. Got it?

CLAIRE. Why are you doing all this packing up and leaving? *(Pause.)* I said why are you doing all this packing up and leaving? *(Pause.)* Click, click, click, go on, click.

MARGOT. From the time we got to Greenwich that's all we did.

CLAIRE. Did what?

MARGOT. Every time you lied, we clicked. It was really sad . . . except for Nonnie. Nonnie laughed a lot. Know why Nonnie laughed a lot? 'Cause no matter how many times she clicked, you never heard her.

CLAIRE. What?

MARGOT. Muffy, Timmy, me. No matter how many times a day we clicked, till we walked in this room just now, you never heard one click.

CLAIRE. That's not true. I heard all the clicking. *(MARGOT clicks twice.)* I only told one lie. Don't make two clicks.

MARGOT. You never once heard the clicking in Greenwich, did you? *(Pause.)* I said, you never once heard the clicking in Greenwich, did you? *(CLAIRE shakes her head no.)* Listen, a room without a click, a rare holiday miracle. *(Pause.)* We'd meet every night and record our clicks. We'd add up how many lies you told each day. You made up three thousand one hundred and eighty-three. Not one day during our stay in Greenwich did you total less than two hundred and eighty clicks. It's unheard of.

(Suddenly the buzzer in the wall buzzes—TWO LONG BUZZES.)

MARGOT. Two minutes to go. Tell me something not a lie. *(Pause.)* Do one, simple not a lie.

CLAIRE. I don't know what you mean.

MARGOT. *(Imitating Nonnie.)* "Liars lie because they are afraid what they really want won't come true. I'm going to make it come true." *(As self.)* Nonnie explains that we're going to build The Power of Rock just like you lied about. *(Imitating Nonnie.)* "I know how to break Claire of her lying! Make one of her lies turn out true."

CLAIRE. And when is she going to do it?

MARGOT. It's already done. Remember the two days after Christmas when your dad and Nonnie went to New York City? Not true, Nonnie bought the place by the river in the turn of the road on Tinker Street. Right now thirty workmen are getting it ready. Claire, you have till June.

CLAIRE. June for what?

MARGOT. To straighten out. If you do, there'll be a job waiting for you. *(BUZZER on wall buzzes two short beeps.)* Last chance. Got anything you want to say? *(Pause.)* Move your mouth. Say some words. Not a lot.

CLAIRE. I . . . want . . . to . . .

MARGOT. To what?

CLAIRE. I . . . want . . . to . . .

MARGOT. I want to get out by June. I want to work with Margot and Nonnie in their Power of Rock Store on Tinker Street. I want to be part of something not a lie.

CLAIRE. *(Shaking her head.)* Yes.

MARGOT. You got to say it yourself.

CLAIRE. What I want will kill the world. My feeling will kill the room. My anger will blow up the bag. I want things the way I see them in my head. I can't put words to them.

MARGOT. *(Kissing Claire on the cheek.)* Then I guess you won't have a job for the summer.

CLAIRE. Please don't go.

(More HONKING from car. MARGOT hands TEDDY BEAR to CLAIRE.)

MARGOT. Teddy will listen if you don't lie.

(MARGOT picks up both suitcases and rushes out of room. CLAIRE sits on bed and tries to talk to bear. Her mouth moves but no words come out. CLAIRE continues to try to talk to bear.)

CLAIRE.   I . . . want . . . to . . . *(Pause.)* I . . . want . . . to . . . *(Pause.)* I . . . want . . . to . . . get . . . out.

(NURSE KASAVA'S voice is heard over the PA system.)

NURSE KASAVA'S VOICE. Emily St. John, where are you hiding? *(Pause.)* Emily, we are starting our emergency search. No patients off their wing floor. *(Pause.)* It is the first day of the New Year. Wisconsin just defeated USC in the Rose Bowl. A forty-six-yard field goal with three seconds to go. I close my eyes and I see us at the front gate, hand in hand, walking down the hill. The music is playing, we're free, we're fine, as long as we stay on the right track and sing the right song. Look at how often Frank has messed up and he's still here.

(Music used on page 16 begins to play on the sound track. CLAIRE listens and laughs.)

CLAIRE. Fuck you, Frank. *(CLAIRE crosses to her tape player and pops in a tape. Music comes up on the track.[8] CLAIRE dances as we fade to BLACK.)*

END OF PLAY

---

[8]See pages 2 & 5 for music information.

COSTUME PLOT

MARGOT
Act I, sc. 1 and 2
Green tweed coat (STRIKE for I, 2)
Patterned knit gloves and hat
Cotton khaki slacks
Grey "thermal knit" cardigan
Short green crochet cardigan
Baby blue cotton turtle neck
Grey sox
Blue slip-on keds

Act I, sc. 3
REPEAT khakis, blue turtle neck, shoes, sox
Multi-colored rayon shirt
RESTORE grey cardigan (if possible)
Eyeglasses

Act I, sc. 4
REPEAT shoes, sox
Jean denim draw-string pants
Oversize white V-neck T-shirt
REPEAT short green cardigan
Act I, sc. 5 STRIKE sweater, shoes

Act I, sc. 6
Brown/green checked slacks
Pale yellow cotton turtle neck
REPEAT grey cardigan, shoes, sox, coat

Act II, sc 1
REPEAT shoes
REPEAT khakis, multi-colored rayon shirt
Royal blue T-shirt
ADD (during scene) maroon cardigan

Act II, sc. 2 STRIKE shirt
REPEAT blue T-shirt, khakis, maroon cardigan, sox
Pale yellow cotton T-shirt

Act II, sc. 3
REPEAT sox, brown/green checked slacks
Bright yellow cotton knit shirt w/ orange knit collar

Act II, sc. 4
Grey w/ red floral pullover sweater
Grey leggings
Black slip-on shoes
REPEAT coat
Plaid scarf
Leather gloves

CLAIRE
Act I, sc. 1
Blue tie-dyed T-shirt
Black/red stripe cotton turtle neck
Multi-colored patchwork shirt
Blue chenille cardigan
Black jeans
Sox
Red fleece-lined slippers
UNDERDRESSED pajama bottoms

Act I, sc. 2
STRIKE black/red T, patchwork shirt, cardigan
ADD yellow flannel shirt

REPEAT slippers, sox
Orange sweat pants
Pink/black stripe boat-neck, long-sleeved T-shirt
Black plaid shirt

Act I, sc. 4
STRIKE pink/black, plaid
REPEAT slippers, sox, sweat pants
ADD black T-shirt w/ yellow eyes
Cut down sweat shirt

Act I, sc. 5 STRIKE sweat shirt, sweat pants
REPEAT slippers, sox; REVEAL pajama bottoms
ADD blue chenille sweater

Act I, sc. 6
REPEAT pajama bottoms, T-shirt, sox
Blue jeans
Short grey tweed pullover sweater
Black tennis shoes

Act II, sc. 1
Black jeans, slippers, sox
Black rayon w/ white stripe shirt, à la Bruce Springsteen
White V-neck T-shirt

Act II, sc. 2
REPEAT orange sweatpants, yellow flannel shirt, slippers,
    sox
Faded purple scoop-neck T-shirt
Black/orange/red checked flannel shirt

Act II, sc. 3
STRIKE checked flannel shirt
REPEAT blue jeans, yellow flannel, faded purple T-shirt,
    slippers, sox
ADD blue chenille sweater

Act II, sc. 4
Blue jeans, sox
Purple/green stripe knit shirt
Black jean jacket
Black motorcycle shoes
patterned, fringed rayon scarf

ALSO BY JOHN FORD NOONAN . . .

SOME MEN NEED HELP. (Little Theatre) Comedy. 2m. Int. This off-beat comedy about male friendship might actually be subtitled "A Coupla White Guys Sitting Around Talking," as it resembles structurally Mr. Noonan's Off-Broadway hit *A Coupla White Chicks.* . . . When we first meet Harley T. Singleton III, he is face down on his suburban kitchen floor, dead drunk. His neighbor, an ex-mafioso named Gaetano Altobelli, is determined to save Harley from himself and is willing to go to any lengths to do so. "It is like a cross between Pinter and Shepard with a little sweetening . . . Pleasing, judiciously proportioned little exercise for two actors."—*N.Y. Daily News.* "A contemporary, oddball version of the Good Samaritan parable . . . A compassionately upbeat theme."—*Christian Science Monitor.*

TALKING THINGS OVER WITH CHEKHOV. (Little Theatre) Comedy. 1m 1f Int. Ext. Jeremy is an aspiring if off-the-wall playwright who draws his inspiration and expertise from extended conversations with Chekhov. Walking in the park, Jeremy encounters his ex-lady Marlene jogging. He has just completed his first play and a production is in the wings. Marlene, formerly an actress who almost won a Tony but retired after her nervous breakdown, determines to rekindle the relationship and play the leading lady in Jeremy's play. The agony of releasing his play to the sharks of theatredom drives Jeremy to induce someone to kill him during rehearsals. He does survive to see his play open, only to have the *New York Times* critic laud Marlene's performance in an insignificant vehicle unworthy of her gifts. "Very amusing . . . Noonan's brand of looniness is unique."—*N.Y. Daily News.* "A joyride . . . funny as hell."—*N.Y. Post.* "One of the funniest, wittiest, exuberant evenings I have spent in the theatre this year."—*Artscene.*

Consult our BASIC CATALOGUE OF PLAYS and/or latest SUPPLEMENT for details.

CEMENTVILLE
by Jane Martin
Comedy
Little Theatre

(5m., 9f.) Int. The comic sensation of the 1991 Humana Festival at the famed Actors Theatre of Louisville, this wildly funny new play by the mysterious author of *Talking With* and *Vital Signs* is a brilliant portrayal of America's fascination with fantasy entertainment, "the growth industry of the 90's." We are in a run-down locker room in a seedy sports arena in the Armpit of the Universe, "Cementville, Tennessee," with the scurviest bunch of professional wrasslers you ever saw. This is decidedly a small-time operation—not the big time you see on TV. The promoter, Bigman, also appears in the show. He and his brother Eddie are the only men, though; for the main attraction(s) are the "ladies." There's Tiger, who comes with a big drinking problem and a small dog; Dani, who comes with a large chip on her shoulder against Bigman, who owes all the girls several weeks' pay; Lessa, an ex-Olympic shotputter with delusions that she is actually employed presently in athletics; and Netty, an overweight older woman who appears in the ring dressed in baggy pajamas, with her hair in curlers, as the character "Pajama Mama." There is the eager-beaver go-fer Nola, a teenager who dreams of someday entering the glamorous world of pro wrestling herself. And then, there are the Knockout Sisters, refugees from the Big Time but banned from it for heavy-duty abuse of pharmaceuticals as well as having gotten arrested *in flagrante delicto* with the Mayor of Los Angeles. They have just gotten out of the slammer; but their indefatigable manager, Mother Crocker ("Of the Auto-Repair Crockers") hopes to get them reinstated, if she can keep them off the white powder. Bigman has hired the Knockout Sisters as tonight's main attraction, and the fur really flies along with the sparks when the other women find out about the Knockout Sisters. Bigman has really got his hands full tonight. He's gotta get the girls to tear each other up in the ring, not the locker room; he's gotta deal with tough-as-nails Mother Crocker; he's gotta keep an arena full of tanked-up rubes from tearing up the joint—and he's gotta solve the mystery of who bit off his brother Eddie's dick last night.   (#5580)

NEW COMEDIES FROM SAMUEL FRENCH, INC.

MAIDS OF HONOR. (Little Theatre.) Comedy. Joan Casademont. 3m., 4f. Comb Int./Ext. Elizabeth McGovern, Laila Robins and Kyra Sedgwick starred in this warm, wacky comedy at Off-Broadway's famed WPA Theatre. Monica Bowlin, a local TV talk-show host, is getting married. Her two sisters, Isabelle and Annie, are intent on talking her out of it. It seems that Mr. Wonderful, the groom-to-be, is about to be indicted for insider trading, a little secret he has failed to share with his fiancee, Monica. She has a secret she has kept herself, too—she's pregnant, possibly not by her groom-to-be! All this is uncovered by delightfully kookie Isabelle, who aspires to be an investigative reporter. She'd also like to get Monica to realize that she is marrying the wrong man, for the wrong reason. She should be marrying ex-boyfriend Roger Dowling, who has come back to return a diary Monica left behind. And sister Annie should be marrying the caterer for the wedding, old flame Harry Hobson—but for some reason she can't relax enough to see how perfect he is for her. The reason for all three Bowlin women's difficulties with men, the reason why they have always made the wrong choice and failed to see the right one, is that they are the adult children of an alcoholic father and an abused mother, both now passed away, and they cannot allow themselves to love because they themselves feel unlovable. Sound gloomy and depressing? No, indeed. This delightful, wise and warm-hearted new play is loaded with laughs. We would also like to point out to all you actors that the play is also loaded with excellent monologues, at least one of which was recently included in an anthology of monologues from the best new plays.)   (#14961)

GROTESQUE LOVESONGS. (Little Theatre.) Comedy. Don Nigro. (Author of *The Curate Shakespeare As You Like It, Seascape with Sharks and Dancer* and other plays). This quirky new comedy about a family in Terre Haute, Indiana, enchanted audiences at NYC's famed WPA Theatre. Two brothers, Pete and John, live with their parents in a big old house with an attached greenhouse. The father, Dan, has a horticulture business. A pretty young woman named Romy is more or less engaged to marry younger brother Johnny as the play begins, and their prospects look quite rosy, for Johnny has just inherited a ton of money from recently-deceased family friend, Mr. Agajanian. Why, wonders Pete, has Agajanian left his entire estate to Johnny? He starts to persistently ask this question to his mother, Louise. Eventually, Louise does admit that, in fact, Mr. Agajanian was Johnny's father. This news stuns Johnny; but he's not *really* staggered until he goes down to the greenhouse and finds Pete and Romy making love. Pete, it seems, has always desperately wanted Romy; but when she chose Johnny instead he married a woman in the circus who turned out to be a con artist, taking him for everything he had and then disappearing. It seems everyone but Johnny is haunted by a traumatic past experience: Louise by her affair with Agajanian; Dan by the memory of his first true love, a Terre Haute whore; Pete by his failed marriage, and Romy by her *two* failed marriages. (One husband she left; the other was run over by a truckload of chickens [He loved cartoons so much, says Romy, that it was only fitting he should die like Wile E. Coyote.]). And, each character but Johnny knows what he wants. Louise and Dan want the contentment of their marriage; Romy wants to bake bread in a big old house—and she wants Pete, who finally admits that he wants her, too. And, finally, Johnny realizes what he wants. He does not want the money, or Agajanian's house. He wants to go to Nashville to make his own way as a singer of sad—yes, grotesque—love songs in the night. NOTE: this play is a treasure-trove of scene and monologue material.)   (#9925)